P9-CDV-245

15-00

Successful Bluefishing

HENRY LYMAN

Successful Bluefishing

International Marine Publishing Company

CAMDEN, MAINE

Contents

Preface

BLUEFISH FASCINATE ME. WHEN I WAS NO higher than a short boat rod, I stared in wonder at the head of a mummichog impaled on the lead hook of a tandem rig. The tail was on the trailing hook. A snapper bluefish had neatly removed the middle section without touching either barb and I could not figure out how this was possible. My father and brother were in the same boat—literally and figuratively —as we drifted across Buttermilk Bay at the base of Cape Cod.

That day marked the beginning of my attempts to learn something about one of the most savage fish that swims the seas. I have learned a little, yet before my line runs out in this angling world, I hope to learn much more.

For the benefit of those who are not familiar with the world of outdoor writing, I would like to explain how and why an individual becomes an "authority" on a particular species of fish. In my own case, it started when the late George Albrecht of Ashaway, Rhode Island, and I were fishing off Block Island. Bluefish—and all other fish for that matter—had avoided us as we trolled, cast, and presented artificial lures in a hundred different ways. Finally we anchored and tried still-fishing with bait. Our conversation had drifted to the reputations of various outdoor writers, good and bad, and we wondered aloud how some had become authorities and experts upon a variety of subjects when, in some cases, the individuals knew very little about the subjects themselves.

"Chances of becoming an authority lie in the oceans," I said. "So little is known today about marine game species that anyone with a minimum of work can become an expert almost overnight."

"You're right," George replied. "Let's capitalize on it. The next fish I catch, I'll set out to become the world's authority on it—and you do the same with anything you catch."

We agreed. George immediately thereafter hooked and boated a very small squirrel hake. My first catch was a snapper bluefish. Since the public appeal of squirrel hake to anglers is not notably high, my chances of achieving recognized expert status were excellent compared to his.

Some years later, in 1950, I wrote a book about bluefish. In late 1951, an article appeared in the *New York Times* which started: "Hal Lyman, the world's authority on bluefish, reports. . . ." I sent the clipping to George and he did not speak to me for a month even though he had an equal chance with squirrel hake. Thus are experts and authorities in angling circles created.

No individual, whether an alleged authority or not, can possibly learn and retain all the available knowledge there is concerning an ocean species. Therefore, I am indebted to countless fishermen, both anglers and commercial men, who have supplied me with information that appears in this volume. In some cases, their names are noted in the text. In others, the names may well have been forgotten or were never even known to me. Formal introductions generally are lacking on the beach. As publisher of *Salt Water Sportsman* magazine, I have received reams of correspondence concerning bluefish and bluefishing. Over the years, I have squirreled away bits and pieces of fact, much of which appears in what follows. I thank all these fellow fishermen and hope they will recognize—and claim—what is their own. I act only as a smelting pot to pour the molten metal of words into a bluefish mold.

Particular thanks are due Frank Woolner—friend, fisherman, hunter, military historian, and a true naturalist in the old sense of the word. As editor of *Salt Water Sportsman,* Frank has faced me across a desk for more years than either one of us likes to remember. We have collaborated on many books and articles, so that what one writes, the other criticizes and rewrites almost instinctively. He reviewed the manuscript of this book, made suggestions for change, and argued with me over basic points. Many of his excellent photographs appear throughout this volume.

For both photographs and sound information, thanks are due also to H. K. "Kib" Bramhall, Jr. and E. R. "Spider" Andresen, advertising director and associate editor respectively of *Salt Water Sportsman.* Both are top notch anglers and both have contributed many ideas and suggestions which are incorporated in this book.

In the scientific world, the rule is to publish or die. For this reason, researchers guard their information closely until such time as they can put it into print for the information of their peers. I am therefore deeply indebted to Dr. Lionel A. Walford, director emeritus of the Sandy Hook Marine Laboratory in Highlands, New Jersey, who not only supplied me with much material yet to be published in scientific journals, but also read and corrected the manuscript on the life history of the species.

The research program undertaken by the Sandy Hook Marine Laboratory under the guidance of Bert Walford is one of the most comprehensive to date on bluefish along the Atlantic Coast. Among the workers on that effort who have supplied me with information, both verbal and written, are Bori L. Olla, Anne L. Studholme, Warren W. Marchioni, Harvey M. Katz, David G. Deuel, and John R. Clark. Without their help, most of the facts concerning the life history of the species would be pure conjecture.

Finally, I must thank my wife, Marjorie. Not a fisherwoman, she has been very patient over many years.

Henry Lyman

Cambridge
Massachusetts

PHOTO CREDITS

Successful Bluefishing

1 / The Fish

SLASHING, SNAPPING, DRIVING FRANTIC BAIT before them in showers of silver, bluefish move through many of the warmer seas of the world as efficient killers—predators supreme. Steamlined, ferocious, often cannibalistic, they are a match for any fish of their own size and more than a match for most. In brief, they are in a class by themselves.

Scientists have recognized this fact. They have placed the species in the family *Pomatomidae* and it is the only member of that family known today. The bluefish's official title of *Pomatomus saltatrix* may be translated as a sheathed, leaping, cutting edge. The name is apt— as many fishermen, bearing scars from the needle-sharp teeth of a bluefish, know to their cost.

Little was known about the life cycle of the species until comparatively recent times. The great naturalist Louis Agassiz thought he had discovered fertilized eggs in the 1860's, hatched them carefully— and ended up with a jar full of silver hake fry! Later, he evidently did isolate free-floating eggs, but his hatching experiments resulted in failure. Agassiz managed to collect what he believed to be bluefish fry from the ocean and described them in detail, but subsequent investigation indicated that he had been working with some other species.

Kib Bramhall hefts a 17-pound bluefish taken off No Mans Land, Massachusetts.

Almost a hundred years later, in 1959, Soviet scientist L.P. Salekhova managed to hatch eggs from ripe roe and milt obtained from spawning bluefish in the Black Sea. She kept the tiny blues alive for five days and published the first accurate description known of such young bluefish. A couple of years later, similar hatching experiments conducted at the Sandy Hook Marine Laboratory in New Jersey, during which the specimens were kept alive even longer, further corroborated what a bluefish looks like in infancy.

For those who like their bluefish very small, let me say that the distinguishing characteristics after they start to look more like a fish than an embryo are bright blue eyes, easily distinguishable dorsal fins, and the start of those death-dealing teeth. Some years ago, I managed to dredge up some of them in a plankton haul net along the shores of Nomans Land off the Massachusetts coast.

I have observed the spawning behavior of bluefish in inshore waters thanks to the late Winslow Warren of Walpole, Mass., and Captain Warren H. Whitehead of Elizabeth City, North Carolina. When I wrote some years ago that no one had discovered spawning grounds of the species, I was informed in a polite way by this angling pair that I was a liar. They had both observed blues multiplying their kind along the southern shore of Nomans Land mentioned above. Since that time, I have observed the same thing and have had several readers of *Salt Water Sports-*

Typical bluefish, built for speed and destructiveness.

Make sure the bluefish is dead before you examine its dental equipment.

man Magazine describe similar activity in the Coney Island area off New York.

Female fish swim slowly along in water usually less than ten feet in depth. They are escorted by several males trailing astern, but I have yet to see more than four males—or presumed males—following one of the opposite sex. The female rolls on her side and extrudes eggs while the males, also rolling at a far more rapid rate, fertilize them. There is no bunting of the female, as is common among some other marine species. While the fish are actually in the process of spawning, I have never been able to hook one.

Even before spawning, the fish are difficult to catch. They seem to prefer a spoon or metal jig at such times, although they will also take underwater plugs and—rarely—surface lures. My guess is that they attack to protect their territory rather than to obtain food. It would be chivalric to think that the males alone did the attacking in defense of their lady love, but such is not the case. I and others have caught fish of both sexes under these conditions. After spawning, blues are ravenous and usually will hit anything offered to them.

As will be noted later, bluefish spawn offshore as well as inshore. However, the inshore grounds known today apparently have similar characteristics—fairly shallow water, broken and rocky bottom, and a sharp drop-off facing the open sea.

In 1960, a modest research effort on bluefish was mounted at the Sandy Hook Marine Laboratory, now operated by the National Marine Fisheries Service, a part of the National Oceanic and Atmospheric Administration in the U.S. Department of Commerce. Although the project started in a small way, it rapidly developed to a coastwide program along the Atlantic shore from New England to Florida. For much of the material that follows concerning the growth of bluefish, their spawning and migrations, I am indebted

to Dr. Lionel A. Walford, former director of the laboratory, and his staff. A great deal of the information below has yet to be published in scientific journals.

Once a baby blue has reached the size at which it can be readily identified, it starts to eat at an extraordinary rate of speed. Snappers, which are young fish weighing less than a pound, jump from eight inches and half a pound to almost 14 inches and better than two pounds in a single year. Weight is nearly doubled in the third year, and a four-year-old averages over six pounds and measures approximately 21 inches.

It should be noted at this point that bluefish between a pound and two pounds in many areas are called tailors, or tailor blues. In some sections of Chesapeake Bay, any bluefish is called a tailor. Just to confuse things further, Australians call *all* bluefish tailors. If you move to South Africa, the name is elf. Among fishermen, there are various local terms, such as Hatteras blues designating specimens taken off the Cape of that name in North Carolina when they weigh five pounds or better. Some Rhode Islanders label snappers as skipjack and, off the Maryland and Virginia coasts, "summer blues" is not the name of a song, but fish weighing from two to three pounds.

American anglers are imaginative and are always dreaming up new terms. "Chopper" has been a bluefish nickname since the early days of angling literature in this country. The reason is obvious. Just watch those bluefish jaws at work! "Slammers" and "jumbos" to designate exceptionally large specimens made a linguistic appearance when the runs of big fish started in the 1960's. Undoubtedly other names will develop over the years, and some may drop from common usage just as the old terms for bluefish such as "snapping mackerel" and "greenfish" have.

Returning to the growth rate, increases

AGE (YEARS)

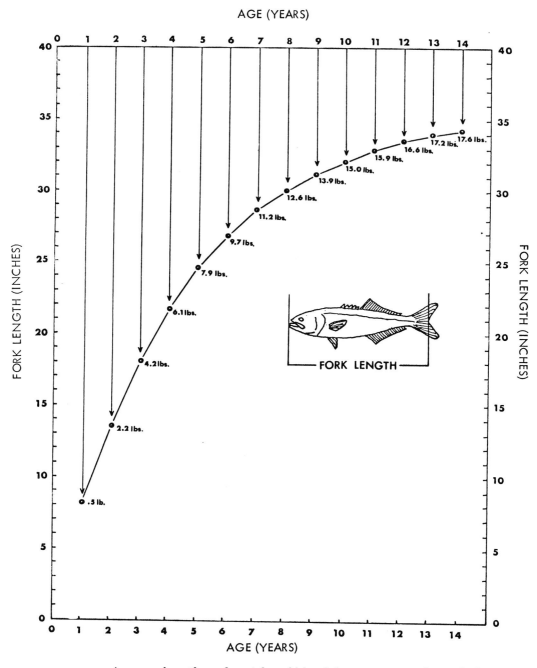

Average length and weight of bluefish at ages one through fourteen.

slow down appreciably after the blue's sixth birthday, at which time individuals weigh almost ten pounds. This slow-down is typical of many marine species. Thus a 15 pounder is about 10 years old and a 17½ pounder, about 14. Just how old the present International Game Fish Association record fish of 31 pounds, 12 ounces, may have been is anyone's guess. This monster was taken on January 30, 1972, by James M. Hussey of Tarboro, North Carolina, and measured 46½ inches. The fish, caught off Hatteras Inlet, displaced the previous record of 24 pounds, 3 ounces, hooked in 1952 off the Azores.

Before leaving Hussey's huge fish, it should also be noted that such specimens may well be considered giants of their kind rather than exceptionally large, normal bluefish. Anglers tend to believe that very large individual game fish of any kind are large simply because they are very old. Rarely is this the case. As a fish ages, it must spend more time catching enough food to maintain itself. Growth rate slows down and, in extreme cases, very old fish actually lose weight in their declining years. If some bright young fisheries scientist were to develop a diet for bluefish that would produce 35-pounders as a regular thing, he would make a fortune.

It may well be that the Hussey bluefish, which is believed to have been about 20 years old, had some sort of glandular trouble which caused it to grow far larger than normal. Physical giants among humans have the same trouble.

I have seen some equivalent monsters off the North African coast taken by local

James Hussey holding his 31-pound, 12-ounce bluefish caught off Hatteras Inlet on the Outer Banks of North Carolina. He made the catch on a plastic eel and 30-pound-test line. The fish shattered a 19-year-old record for the largest bluefish according to the IGFA.

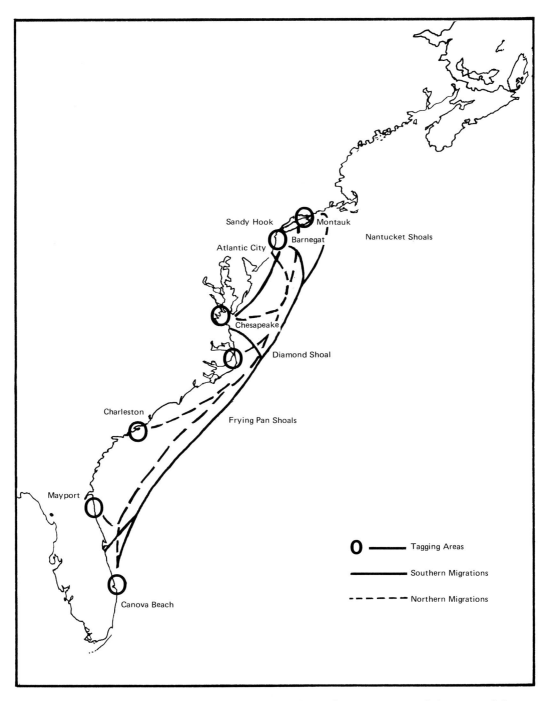

Bluefish migrations along the east coast of the United States.

commercial fishermen, who normally drift a live bait on a handline, then, when the blue has been hooked, let it fight the light dhow—a locally made small boat—until exhausted. Phil Mayer of New York City reported to me that he saw a 45 pounder taken in this manner. This would appear to be close to the maximum weight for the species.

Up until the middle of the last century, there were many fishermen who believed sincerely that snapper blues were a completely different species than their adult brethren. The younger fish with large heads and small bodies, and the adults with these characteristics reversed, gave rise to this theory. In addition, the appearance of the two age groups at widely different times of year on many sections of the coast supported the myth. Marine biologists long since have exploded this particular fantasy, but there certainly is some question about the different populations, or races, of blues. Here, things become complicated.

Taxonomists apparently enjoy dividing species into sub-species and giving each group a different name. I deplore this muddying of the classification waters and will try to outline the general habits of the distinct races, their life cycles and characteristics. All will not agree with me. For example, William A. Lund, working at the University of Cornell, claimed there are six individual races of blues along the Atlantic coast alone. His findings are based on gill raker counts of young fish. Just how all six of these races keep from interbreeding and mingling is not explained. Gill rakers, by the way, are bony filaments on the fish's bronchial arch, and the number of them is referred to as the count.

A Sandy Hook research team spent about a half hour per fish taking all sorts of measurements on the bluefish year classes of 1962 and 1968. The samples totalled several hundred specimens. These measurements were all cranked into a

computer and, when the final calculations were completed, it appeared that one race, called the "northern summer spawners" for ease of reference, basically have smaller heads than another, labelled the "southern spring spawners." Remember these two races, for I plan to refer to each many times. There is a possibility that there is an additional Florida race on the United States coast, but data is not sufficient to pin this down accurately.

The southern spring spawning race apparently procreates from early spring into June at the edge of the Gulf Stream. The young then drift north under the influence of the Gulf Stream current and are carried past Cape Hatteras up toward New England. On this northbound trip, schools peel off from the main body of fish and travel westward to show up as snappers in the area from New Jersey to New England. By fall, the fish of the two races are of different sizes, with those of the spring spawners naturally being much larger than those of the northern summer spawners. Obviously they have a time advantage during which they eat as only bluefish can.

It appears that the southern-spawned fish then move south via an offshore route as the waters cool. They contribute to the winter fishery in Florida. The next year, they head north again and appear all along the coast, concentrating in New England, New York, and New Jersey in particular. However, as this race grows in age and size, these blues seem to show up less and less in inshore catches. It may well be that they are basically oceanic in nature. There is even a possibility that some of them actually cross the Atlantic, although this has yet to be proved.

The progeny resulting from the summer spawning move southward past Hatteras and evidently spend their first winter offshore. The following spring, they move into estuarine waters—primarily the sounds of North Carolina—where they remain until fall. In subsequent years, they summer in northern waters.

The northern summer spawners make up the bulk of the bluefish which spawn close to the coast. They reproduce first in the early summer and may continue to spawn well into August. It is common angling knowledge that blues appear in the northern part of their range as early as May in some years, are fat and fussy in their feeding when they first arrive, then apparently vanish for a couple of weeks— only to reappear again, gaunt, hungry, and mean, in midsummer. These fish have taken a holiday to procreate. As noted earlier, some of their spawning grounds are known, but many remain to be discovered along much of the northeast coast.

The relative number of northern- and southern-spawned bluefish varies from year to year. This undoubtedly reflects differences in infant mortality resulting from vagaries of water temperatures, currents, and available food around at the respective times and areas of their hatching.

Young of the northern summer spawners move south in the fall and spend their first winter somewhere off the Carolinas, for they move into the sounds of that area in their second season. These sounds provide excellent nurseries, and it is obvious that their preservation is of primary concern for the future of both races of bluefish. From that time onward, the northerners apparently follow in general a south-to-north route in the spring and summer, and a north-to-south path in the fall. Just how far offshore they move and how far south they go is still a matter for conjecture.

Although tagging of blues has resulted in much more knowledge concerning their migrations being obtained, there is still much work to be done before all the answers are supplied. Tagging itself presents a problem. In years gone by, I have tagged specimens with the Petersen disc-

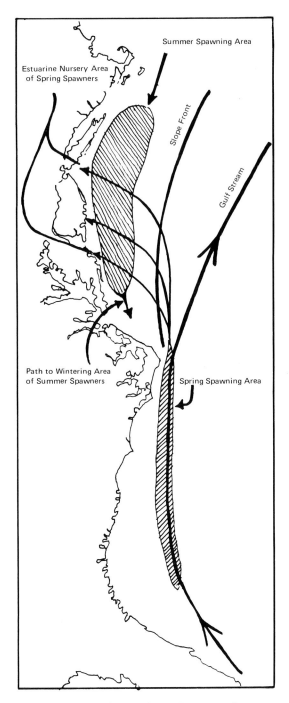

Movements of bluefish during their early life along the east coast of the United States.

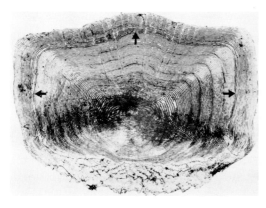

Bluefish scale with a large first annulus.

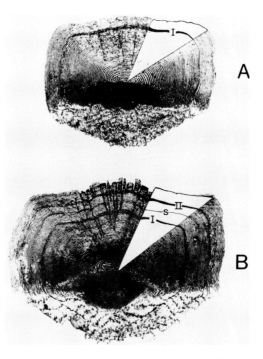

Bluefish scales: A. Taken at time of tagging, showing one annulus (I). B. Returned one year later, showing a second annulus (II) and a scar from the tagging operation.

type marker—two circular bits of plastic held together by a pin thrust through the flesh of the fish. Unfortunately, such a tag evidently looks good to eat, and the decorated blues were attacked by their fellows when returned to the water. Tags are normally placed just to the rear of the dorsal fin, so an attack on the tag means serious injury to the fish. Today tags are of the spaghetti type, but there still may be some similar mortality.

That tagging is a shock to individual fish is evident from a study of the scales. Adult bluefish add an annulus mark on their scales every year, much as a tree adds rings on a cross-section of its trunk. When a fish is tagged, a false annulus appears. Humans often grow a ridge on their fingernails after a particularly violent or emotional disturbance. Bluefish apparently feel the same way about being tagged.

Although studies to date explain migrations of two races of western Atlantic Ocean bluefish, explanations of their movements elsewhere around the world are still a mystery. In the 1850's and again in the late summer and early autumn of 1971, blues were abundant as far north as Old Orchard Beach, Maine. Rarely, a stray will swim to the waters of southern Nova Scotia, evidently enticed there by some wandering eddy of the Gulf Stream current. Basically, they are taken from Massachusetts to Florida in the eastern United States. There is a considerable population of small fish in the southern part of the Gulf of Mexico and, in some seasons, even in the upper part of the Gulf.

Although only one or two specimens have been recorded off Bermuda, in the Caribbean to the south—particularly off Cuba—the species is common seasonally. Dr. Ruben Jaen of Caracas, in his book *Fishing in the Caribbean,* reports that bluefish *(anchoa)* abound around the island of Margarita, which lies off Punta Arenas in Venezuela, during February and March, disappear for a time, then return in July and August. They appear off the coast of Uruguay in April and May and, further north, off the coast of Brazil during June. Perhaps this is another race which has adapted itself to warmer wa-

Kay Townsend of Shrewsbury, Massachusetts, with a good-sized bluefish.

ters. Catches in commercial quantities are made off Argentina also, which seems to support this speculation.

Across the Atlantic, bluefish range from the Azores and the coast of Portugal southwards to, and around, the Cape of Good Hope in Africa. By this I do not mean that they can be taken all through the year along the entire west coast of Africa. Their movements are seasonal, and the seasons closely parallel those of fish found between Massachusetts and Florida—good fishing in the north during summer and fall, good fishing in the south during the winter.

Migrations also pass through the Strait of Gibraltar and into the Mediterranean.

Whether these blues are part of the African population or form a Mediterranean population of their own is anyone's guess. I opt for the latter, for I have taken blues off the North African shore as well as far to the east near Sicily.

The Black Sea population may also be of different stock. Dr. Walford feels that these blues may move seasonally between the Black Sea itself and the Sea of Marmara to the south. In my opinion, these fish may also slop over to some extent into the Mediterranean.

Fisheries literature over a long period of years cites the Red Sea as another area in which bluefish are found. Despite a diligent search, I have been unable to find any firsthand reports in support of this statement. In many reference works, there is a tendency to pick up information previously published by a presumed authority and to reprint it verbatim without checking on its veracity. In one case, I checked an account of weakfish being taken far offshore in a commercial dragger haul and found the operator of the dragger in fact identified the fish as bluefish. The first erroneous report, however, appeared in five separate scientific papers. I therefore am highly suspicious of the Red Sea as a haven for blues.

In the Pacific, bluefish are limited in range primarily to the eastern and western coasts of Australia, Tasmania, and the Tasman Sea, which lies between Australia and New Zealand. Trevor D. Scott in his book *The Marine and Fresh Water Fishes of South Australia* states: "The record of this species for South Australia is unsatisfactory and requires verification." In any case, Aussie anglers make the most of tailor runs. After dark near Brisbane in the winter—June, July, and August in those latitudes—they make the fishing a sort of family outing, complete with fillets cooked over an open fire.

Again reference books claim that blues are found in the eastern part of the Indian

Ocean around the Malay Peninsula. Confusion with native names undoubtedly distorts the record, but I have been unable to find any sound basis for this statement. Dr. Lionel A. Walford has called my attention to a catch reported from Ambon, just west of Dutch New Guinea, that is mentioned in *Fishes of the Indo-Australian Archipelago* by Weber and De Beaufort. It is evident that bluefish are merely strays in that part of the world.

On the western side of the Indian Ocean, however, there are definite records of catches in the Madagascar area. Presumably, these fish are part of the South African stock.

Many millions of years ago during the Devonian age of fishes, bluefish might have evolved in the Atlantic when the continents were comparatively close together. Geophysicists now believe that North America separated from Europe and environs, and South America separated from Africa even more rapidly—if 100,000,000 years of continental drift can be considered rapid. If this is true, it may explain distribution of bluefish. They could have run around the end of Africa and reached Australia. If they tried do the same thing around the tip of South America, they would have been discouraged by a blast of cold water which caused them to avoid most of the Pacific. This of course is pure conjecture—and was a good deal before my time!

No matter where they may be found, blues swim in much the same manner throughout the world. They keep swimming from the time of birth until death. They cannot rest, stationary, as can many other marine species that even lie in a partially comatose state, as forward motion is required to keep water moving over their gills. Snappers will stick together in rather tightly packed schools so that, if you find one snapper, you will find many others. As the individual fish grow, they tend to spread out to cover a wider area.

When they approach the ten-pound mark, the number of individuals in a school drops. Often these larger specimens will be in groups of only a half dozen, or even may be loners.

In my own fishing, I have never noted that particular schools of blues are made up of one sex only. However, A.J.McLane, executive editor of *Field and Stream* magazine and one of the country's top anglers, does a good deal of bluefishing in the Palm Beach section of Florida and has reported the contrary to me. One winter day, he caught four big blues to a top of almost 12 pounds and all were males. On subsequent trips, even larger specimens were taken and all were of that same sex. This may indicate that the larger blues separate by sexes at some time in their life cycle.

Separation of maimed or injured fish is well known off the coast of Hatteras, North Carolina. Every year both commercial and sport fishermen take scarred individuals from schools that arrive about two weeks ahead of the major migrations. The lame and the blind evidently stick together with some sort of fishy understanding that they will not chew on one another.

Bori L. Olla, who watched bluefish held in a huge tank at the Sandy Hook Marine Laboratory on a day-and-night basis, has told me some fascinating tales about their schooling behavior. There is a definite pecking order among individuals in the school, and one ends up as leader. If a new fish is introduced to the group, battles may result until the leader establishes its position as boss. When one blue lags behind the school regularly, the leader often will make a quick circle to the rear and nip the tail of the laggard.

At one point during this fish-watching experiment, Bori Olla saw an unfortunate bluefish whack its nose against the glass of the aquarium; it was momentarily stunned. As it sank slowly, it was torn to pieces in a matter of seconds by its alleged friends. Even in the wild, such cannibalism is not unusual. On several occasions, I have found entire caudal fins lopped from a bluefish in the belly of one of its companions I have caught. Whether such attacks are made intentionally, or unintentionally when in a feeding frenzy, no one knows. At any rate, there is no question that big blues will gobble down smaller ones without any feeling for family and friends. In the Azores, a snapper is a common bait when fishing for jumbo bluefish. There is little wonder that the Hatteras "hospital" schools stick together!

No account of bluefish would be complete without citing the writings of Professor Spencer F. Baird made in 1874 in the report of the United States Commission on Fish and Fisheries. Authors have used the quotation below—with and without credit to the original author—have paraphrased it, and have lifted sentences from it freely. I feel that it can stand on its own merits.

> There is no parallel in the point of destructiveness to the bluefish among the marine species on our coast, whatever may be the case among some of the carnivorous fish of the South American waters. The bluefish has been likened to an animated chopping-machine, the business of which is to cut to pieces and otherwise destroy as many fish as possible in a given space of time. All writers are unanimous in regard to the destructiveness of bluefish. Going in large schools, in pursuit of fish not much inferior to themselves in size, they move along like a pack of hungry wolves, destroying everything before them. Their trail is marked by fragments of fish and by the stain of blood in the sea as, where the fish is too large to be swallowed entire, the hinder portion will be bitten off and the anterior part allowed to float away or sink. It is even maintained with great earnest-

> ness that such is the gluttony of the fish that, when the stomach becomes full, the contents are disgorged and then again filled.

Professor Baird evidently did not believe the last sentence, and neither do I. The idea may have been generated by the fact that blues often regurgitate their latest meal when hooked or netted just before they are beached or boated. Many other species do the same.

There is no question that bluefish will eat just about anything found in the areas in which they swim provided that an edible piece of the creature can be bitten off. To list all the species of marine creatures that have been found in bluefish stomachs would take pages. Even bottom feeding species are not safe from attack. In the *Marine Fisheries Review,* an account of blues chomping happily on yellowtail flounder, accompanied by some unusual photos of flatfish that survived even with large chunks missing from their anatomy, is detailed by Fred E. Lux and John V. Mahoney. At the time of the Civil War, there were many reports of bluefish driving every swimming creature from the waters of Boston Harbor. In brief, a hungry blue will tackle anything at hand until something more tasty swims along.

There is one exception. Despite many reports during World War II that bluefish attacked downed aviators and injured seamen off the North African coast, I can state flatly that this never happened. I personally traced some of these rumors down at the time and all were just that— rumors. No such attack has ever been documented, nor have any eye-witnesses ever been reported. Note, however, that blues will slash a human thumb, toe, or other piece of anatomy when given the chance while being unhooked. This is the only species of true fish—not shark—I have found that will take definite aim at a presumed enemy even when out of the

Al Caputo of Dedham, Massachusetts, with a fine specimen.

water. I have scars to prove it.

At times, bluefish can become highly selective in their feeding habits. A clue to one reason for such selectivity was given in the June, 1970, issue of *Copeia,* a scientific journal which cannot be considered standard bedtime reading for anglers. Bori L. Olla, Harvey M. Katz, and Anne L. Studholme, researchers and fish-watchers at Sandy Hook, wrote an article entitled "Prey Capture and Feeding Motivation in the Bluefish," and it was based on observations made at the tank previously mentioned in the Sandy Hook Marine Laboratory.

Without going into all the details, let me outline the findings. Bluefish were swimming in a school in the tank. Food, in the form of live mummichogs—called killifish in many areas—was tossed into the tank. The individual live baits were small in size. When they hit the water, the bluefish broke out of their schooling formation and started to swim more rapidly than previously.

When an individual bluefish sighted a mummichog, its eyes would turn forward and it would head full steam toward the victim. If it missed, it would turn, slow down, and start searching for another mummichog. Lesson number one for the angler: if a blue misses your lure, present it again in the same area just as soon as possible.

If the bluefish did not miss, it opened its jaws, arched its head, and gobbled the

Stones taken from the stomach of a 7½-pound bluefish, which had also swallowed about 50 small bait fish. Compare the stones with the 1/0 hook. The myth that bluefish swallow sand for ballast in a storm may have started when such stones were found in the fishes' bellies.

minnow down. Immediately, it would turn 90 to 180 degrees from the direction of attack; then, after swallowing the prey, would move back into the area where the food was first found. Again, this indicates that a fisherman should cast or troll over the same water even after a fish has been caught. There may be others that were beaten to the target.

After the bluefish had been satiated with a full meal of small mummichogs, they tended to stop searching for more food in the same area and returned in general to a schooling formation at slower swimming speed. However, when bait of larger size was then introduced into the tank, the bluefish went back to the attack —evidently polishing off the meal with a heavy dessert. The obvious lesson for the angler is: when strikes fall off among a feeding school of blues, switch to a larger lure or natural bait. According to the researchers, chances of success are increased by as much as 90 percent—if fish in the open ocean behave as they did in the tank. It seems highly probable that they would behave in the same manner, for the specimens in the Sandy Hook aquarium were not exposed to the sight of their keepers.

Food supply of course influences local movements of bluefish in any coastal area once the main migrations have arrived. They will not stay in an area that is a biological desert and tend to congregate where bait is readily available. I will go into this in more detail when discussing the best waters for fishing. Just how much effect the food supply has on the migrations themselves is unknown. My personal opinion is that the effect is minimal, for blues can forage on almost anything available.

Temperature, however, has a major

Frank Woolner with a balanced catch of striped bass and bluefish.

effect on these migrations and also on the activity of the fish themselves. In captivity, the lower limit of tolerance among bluefish appears to be about 52 degrees Fahrenheit. In the wild, they apparently can stand water nearly ten degrees colder. When the thermometer reaches 85, blues show signs of extreme distress and try to move elsewhere. Their ideal appears to be about 68 degrees. Obviously, therefore, if a cold current below 60 hangs off a portion of the coast, bluefish will avoid it in favor of something more to their liking.

In studying geographical ranges in which the fish travel and water temperatures—the classic approach to research on marine species—temperatures played an important part in the Sandy Hook research. However, Dr. Walford feels that something else is involved also. It might well be light, which is known to influence migrations of other fish species, birds, and even movements of various mammals.

Light effects have been studied on what might be termed a day-to-day basis. Let me return once again to that Sandy Hook tank with Bori Olla and Anne Studholme watching thermometers, clocks, computers, and bluefish. The aquarium was linked to a lighting system which made it possible to change the duration of artificial daylight, thus simulating not only day and night hours, but also changes in these over a long period of time to indicate a change in the season of the year.

The researchers are very cautious in their conclusions, as befits scientists, but basically they discovered several points. First, bluefish tend to school together and swim more rapidly during daylight hours than during darkness, hence are more active when the sun is up. In addition, activity was increased at the most rapid rate "from the last hourly reading before light onset to the first reading after light onset." In brief, go fishing just before daylight and fish from sunset into the first hour of night. I and thousands of others have found this to be an excellent basic rule while bluefishing. Finally, it appeared that bluefish have a built-in time clock of some sort, so that they can determine the hours of dawn and dusk even when the light stimulus is removed. Again, anglers will agree, for fish in the wild will hit best during those hours even when the sky is covered with heavy clouds which obliterate the sun. This time clock evidently operates to some degree also with respect to seasonal migrations.

All natural conditions cannot be duplicated in a laboratory tank. At times, bluefish in the ocean will feed ravenously in the dead of night. When I first became an avid surf fisherman for blues, my mentors—Ollie Rodman, Doc Johnston, and Fran Davis—pointed out that fishing stopped at Great Point, Nantucket, when it became totally dark. Experience in those by-gone days proved them to be correct. A few years later, the blues changed their habits and were taken all night long. Frank Woolner tells of a long night in 1971, off Cape Cod, when he caught blues in the 12- to 17-pound weight range all night long. The fish hit surface plugs, and they stopped hitting with the first pale light of dawn. In brief, never say always!

If the complicated migratory game of musical chairs along the Atlantic seaboard is only vaguely understood, it still can be classified as crystal clear when compared to the causes of the wild fluctuations in the abundance of bluefish in the same area over a period of years. These cycles of plenty and scarcity were first described by Zaccheus Macy in his *Account of Nantucket:* "From the first coming of the English to Nantucket (1659), a large fal-fish, called the blue-fish, thirty of which would fill a barrel, was caught in great plenty around the Island from the 1st of the sixth month till the middle of the ninth month. But it is remarkable that in the year 1764 . . . they had

all disappeared and that none have ever been taken since. This has been a great loss to us."

Over the years, I have tried to determine just what a "fal-fish" might be, but have had no success. At any rate, if the blues taken by the Nantucketers of that era from June into September ran 30 to the English barrel, they must have weighed 12 to 15 pounds apiece.

Tracing the rise and decline of cycles as far as bluefish are concerned is difficult, because these cycles varied widely on different sections of the coast. Indeed there is good argument that the word "cycle" should not be used at all, because it means something very periodic, and there has never been anything very periodic about the rise and fall of blues. When the fish are abundant off New Jersey, for example, they may well be scarce in Massachusetts.

Variations in water temperature may be a contributing factor, but cannot explain fully the fluctuations in the bluefish supply. Blame has also been attached to the lack of bait as can be illustrated by the following quotation from a fascinating article published in the January 6, 1883, weekly edition of *The American Angler.* The author, who called himself Old Isaak, was on board the sloop *Katy* sailing from New York City to Fire Island. "The water was perfectly alive with fish (be it remembered this was twelve years ago)," he wrote. "The fish-oil factories had not cleaned out the menhaden, the food-fish *par excellence* of all salt water game fish. I repeatedly killed bluefish and mossbunkers on the surface with my revolver. Yet the high, but comparatively smooth sea, made me often send lead in vane. With a shotgun, I could have killed hundreds of mossbunkers in an hour."

Old Isaak's trip, it should be noted, was liberally laced with dippings from jugs of whiskey and rum, and apparently all of his companions were armed to the teeth.

*Trolling for bluefish before the advent of the powerboat. The fishermen are using
artificial squids.*

Such a venture I am always glad to avoid!

In addition to temperature fluctuations and bait supplies, the abundance of other marine species—or lack of it—has also been linked with bluefish cycles. Some claim that, when weakfish are scarce, blues are plentiful and *vice versa*. In examining records, this has been true in some years, completely untrue in others. The every-so-many-years theorists in times gone by claimed that every seven, twelve, fourteen—or you name it—number of years bluefish vanished along the coast. Records again explode this type of statement. In brief, trying to explain the ups and downs with data available at the present time seems to be impossible.

After Macy's account of the disappearance of blues in 1764, the Nantucket Indi-ans began to disappear also and were apparently smitten by some sort of plague. Corollation between American Indian populations and that of bluefish falls apart thereafter. For about 20 years following, the fish were absent, then began to reappear in small numbers. I should emphasize once again that blues may well have been taken in quantity along other sections of the coast during this period. However, records for Massachusetts are more complete over the years from Colonial times than elsewhere, and I cite them simply to show when the fluctuations took place.

Around 1810, blues were abundant south of Cape Cod, moved north of the Cape by 1837 and, in the 1850's, were everywhere even as far north as the Maine coast. The peak of this glut appears to have been reached in 1863 or 1864. Incidentally, no one has ever determined the exact number of blues necessary to make a glut, but the term has been used for years to indicate occasions when the species is extremely plentiful.

By 1889, the fish had declined in numbers. However, according to Henry B. Bigelow and William C. Schroeder, writing in the classic reference work *Fishes of the Gulf of Maine,* some fish were taken in that year as far north and east as Mount Desert Island off the Maine coast. Then a decline set in, but blues continued to be taken north of Cape Cod up until 1910, even though the supply south of the Cape diminished radically. Water temperature may well have played a part.

There were various minor fluctuations for the next decade, but fishing was at a comparatively low ebb until 1927. After a slight increase in the early 1930's, the fishery all but vanished until 1947, when snappers appeared in great numbers. By 1951, bluefish had reached glut proportions, although individual specimens rarely topped the seven-pound mark. With minor dips and peaks in the supply, there appears to have been a more or less steady increase all through the 1960's, and the fish were growing larger and larger.

By 1969, an angler taking a 15 pounder— a catch that would have made headlines in the 1950's—considered he had done nothing unusual. Size and quantities increased and, although the glut was not as spectacular in 1972 off the Massachusetts coast as it was in 1971, an ample supply of small fish augured well for the future. When 1973 rolled around, the blues were back and arrived early—and so it goes on.

Along the Atlantic Coast, 121,000,000 pounds of bluefish were taken by anglers in 1970, according to an angling survey made by the Bureau of the Census for the National Marine Fisheries Service. This catch exceeded that made by commercial fishermen to a considerable degree.

Catches of freak bluefish characterized by physical deformities reach a peak when there is a glut. Pug-nosed specimens, with the upper jaw apparently missing; those with duplicate or deformed fins; and other unusually marked and shaped individuals cause amazement in the angling world. In a normal year, presumably the few freaks produced in the spawning areas do not survive, or survive in such small numbers they are not taken by fishermen. When the base population increases markedly, the number of freaks does also.

Cycles of abundance and scarcity may also be influenced to some degree by parasites in, and on, the bluefish. Like most marine species, blues are subject to attack or infestation by all sorts of creeping, burrowing creatures that can, in some cases, kill their hosts. Obviously such parasites increase when the number of hosts increases. It should be noted that the majority of such parasites are found inside the body cavity of bluefish, and therefore do not taint the flesh as far as human consumption is concerned. Even the few that actually burrow into the flesh are rendered harmless by proper cooking.

There is one long, unpleasant, wormlike critter that appeared in great numbers during the 1960's in the roe sacs of female blues. This worm apparently rendered the eggs of the fish useless, for the roe sacs that had been attacked hardened into a stiff mass. A similar infestation throughout the whole bluefish world naturally would result in spawning failure. Spawning success of course is the basic reason for the fluctuations in supply. Since no one knows just what requirements are needed to produce a dominant year class that will keep the fishery going over a period of years, speculation in this area is futile.

My own particular theory to explain the present abundance of bluefish during the

Deformed bluefish. The fish above with a triple caudal fin was taken by Frank Woolner at Cape Canaveral, Florida, in 1957. The fish below has a humped back caused by a malformation of the spine.

early 1970's—or to explain it in part—is neither patented nor even, perhaps, realistic. However, I submit that fishing effort, both sport and commercial, has increased substantially during the past decade. This means that more fish have been removed from the ocean so that the total population has been kept at a more stable level. As a result, the tremendous gluts of the past have never been realized. Nature's balancing act among food supplies, parasites, and diseases has been kept approximately level. The result: plenty of bluefish over a long period.

I am the first to admit that this theory might be shot full of holes, but it is as good as, and perhaps better than, other explanations which have been offered. Note also that this theory certainly would not apply to other less predacious marine species. Blues are among the few fishes which literally can eat their own way to destruction by depleting the food supply.

One final gem of information before discussing the waters in which bluefish are found: the species is left-eyed. This means that, all other factors being equal, a bluefish will approach its potential meal normally with his left eye focused on it first. This means that, if an angler has a choice, he should present his lure to that same eye if possible.

When I mentioned this rather unusual fact to Bernard "Lefty" Kreh, who was then head man with the Metropolitan Miami Fishing Tournament, he was not at all surprised. Evidently Florida charter boat skippers also have found that billfish are left-eyed. Lefty, who is left-handed, but right-eyed, reported that a bait presented to the left side of a sighted billfish was taken far more readily than one presented to the right side of the same fish.

Left-eyed, right-eyed, or ambi-optic, it makes little difference to me. I plan to keep fishing for blues until they are no longer with us or until I am unable to hold a rod. The latter condition will pertain long before the former.

2 / The Waters

THE CREST CURLING IN A HISS OF FOAM, A wave rolls towards the shore, breaks with a muffled rumble, then sucks back seaward in the trough, carrying countless particles of sand with it as it retreats. Tiny mole crabs, sand fleas, and a host of other creatures living at the ocean's edge burrow frantically to maintain a fragile hold on their shifting home site. If swept to sea, death in the form of a hunting predator awaits, and the small predator in turn may be gobbled down by a larger one at any moment.

Add to this miniature scene of marine carnage flocks of seagulls and terns, scampering shorebirds dipping their bills in the wash with the speed of sewing machine needles, and there is good reason to understand why the life expectancy of miniscule ocean organisms is short. The cycle of eat and be eaten has gone on for eons.

Basic in the food chain of the sea is plankton—micro-organisms of all sorts, which include algae, eggs of sea creatures, bits of plant life both dead and alive, and a host of diatoms. These last form the link between plants and animals in the ocean environment. Their own life span often may be measured in hours. When they die, their minute skeletons form kieselguhr, which contributes to the layers of sediment on the sea floor. I include this interesting bit of information for the benefit of those who, like myself, are fascinated by words and tend to collect bits of trivia with which to startle their friends.

Flowering diatoms—those that are in the process of reproducing their kind—help the bluefisherman. They are the cause of the bluefish "smell," a distinctive odor that may be sniffed at the range of a mile or more when the wind is right. Newcomers to the ocean scene often scoff at the old-time sniffer. When trying to find good water, you should never neglect your sense of smell.

Years ago, James R. Bartholomew, scientist, poet, and fisherman, then connected with the old Farlow Herbarium at Harvard University, described this luscious scent in *Salt Water Sportsman* magazine. "Plankton, like Chanel No. 5, has a bouquet all its very own," he wrote. "It is like a cross between a pea soup fog on the Grand Banks and a crate of honeydew melons. It is fishy, but not too fishy. It is clean, too fresh, with a hint of musky sweetness that no fish ever has until it is sizzling in the frypan with pork scraps and a touch of Madeira."

I cannot improve upon this description. However, in recent years, I have questioned seriously whether this particular plankton bloom attracts small bait and therefore attracts the blues to the area. I have a feeling that the fish themselves produce the plankton, oil, or whatever it may be. Others with whom I have talked agree with me after I have given my arguments.

Let me cite an example in support of this theory. While driving down the outer beach of Great Point on Nantucket Island —which is a prime bluefishing area—

The famed Great Point Rip, Nantucket, Mass.

Francis W. Davis and I were keeping a sharp lookout for working terns or other indications of activity. Fran Davis, the inventor of power steering and one who has taught me much about surf casting, suddenly rolled the car to a stop. Fifty yards offshore, an oily slick bubbled to the surface, spread rapidly, and the air was filled with the fragrance of cucumbers, melons, Madeira, and what-have-you. Bluefish, without question.

Jumping out of the car and grabbing our surf rods from the roof rack, we aimed two metal jigs in the direction of the slick. After two cranks of the reel, Fran was fast to a blue. I, in my excitement, was busily engaged in trying to

clear a backlash! Fortunately, I did so in a matter of moments, cast successfully, and also was hooked to an angry blue in a few seconds.

Now that slick, with its characteristic odor, had come to the surface in the short time required to spot it while we were driving the beach at about 15 miles per hour. I submit that, if the plankton bloom took place at that moment, bluefish would not have had the speed necessary to vector in to the area within the limited number of minutes available.

In addition, if flowering diatoms with this particular scent attract bait, which in turn attract blues, why are not other species equally attracted? Striped bass, weakfish, bonito, channel bass, and many other species are often found in the same waters. It seems logical that they would gather around the same slicks, but normally do not do so until long after the skim on the surface has been widely dissipated. Note also that several of the species give off characteristic odors of there own, with and without slicks. Frank Woolner has theorized that every species may leave a scent trail of sorts, just as a bounding cottontail leaves a trail for a beagle on land. I think he has a point.

Since my experience on Nantucket many years ago, I have studied this phenomenon with more than passing interest. Although visual and olfactory evidence may remain for some time, bluefish appear to be in the immediate vicinity the moment a slick appears. They apparently cause it by the release of some sort of oil. I assumed at one time that it might be caused by their regular excretions, but such evidently is not the case. I have taken the contents of the lower intestine from many specimens, dropped this into water and neither a slick nor the characteristic scent results.

I have even gone so far as to scoop up some of the floating scum—for want of a better word—and have examined it under magnification. Plankton certainly is visible in considerable quantity, yet there appears to be an oily substance mingled with the various diatoms. I am no chemist and am unable to analyze this material, but some angling laboratory man might make himself famous if he did so. Who knows? The substance might be produced artificially to become the finest bluefish attractor known!

Before leaving the subject of bluefish slicks, let me say that it is best to cast or troll to one edge of the oily area rather than the middle. You may well take a fish if you hit dead center, but your chances of taking a second are reduced greatly, for the hooked blue's activity tends to cause

the line to hit others and the school may well be spooked.

Aside from the observation of slicks and the sniffing of them, visual indications of bluefish are many. Obviously good fishing water is where the slashers can be seen. Oddly enough, many anglers do not identify what they are seeing. Time after time, I have watched boatmen speed at full throttle in the direction of breaking fish only to discover upon arrival that they are not bluefish at all.

There are many species of both bait and sport fishes which feed at, or near, the surface. The eruption of a bluefish school, however, is distinctive. Blues appear to hit bait from all angles and over a fairly wide area. Most important, they attack almost simultaneously so that the water appears to explode. To duplicate this phenomenon momentarily, fire a shotgun loaded with number 4 shot into the water at a range of about 30 yards. The shot string will not leap in showers of silver as bait fish do, but the water surface will look much like that during a bluefish attack.

Menhaden and mackerel ripple the surface. Weakfish and striped bass cause more commotion, but the water does not turn white in a moment to calm down sometimes only a few seconds later. Pollock are more sedate and slow-moving than blues when harrying feed on the surface. The same is true of members of the jack family in southern climes. Bonito, to me at least, come closer to duplicating the flurry made by blues at a distance, yet, at closer range, they are easily distinguished from the toothed killers. No matter how much I might write on this subject, it would be impossible to describe the exact appearance of a bluefish school on the surface. The knack of making quick identification comes only through long experience. Even the most experienced, including me, are fooled at times.

If you can cover the water through

which a school of feeding bluefish has passed, it is easy to determine their identity. Bits of bait, injured bait fish, and blood will be much in evidence. Chances are good that the blues will not be far away.

Let me say at this point that the practice of chasing bluefish schools along a beach or with a boat can be one of the most frustrating experiences in angling. The cusses will surface for a short time, then sound at the crucial moment, only to appear again in a minute hundreds of yards away. In such circumstances, I strongly recommend that you stay where you are. Chances are good that the feeding fish will return within a reasonable period.

There are exceptions. Dr. Malcolm K. Johnston, now of Temple, New Hampshire, was among the first in modern times to develop surf fishing for blues in Massachusetts to a fine art. He often told me of sighting a school off the beach at Monomoy Point, which forms the southern spur of Cape Cod. As the fish approached in a strong current running parallel to the shore, he cast, hooked up, fought, and landed a fine specimen. Bait had been carried down current about 50 yards during this procedure, so he sprinted in the soft sand, cast again into the school, and again hooked another of his quarry. This process was repeated five times, at which point Doc collapsed, exhausted, on the sand. I chuckled when he first told this tale. Two years later in exactly the same place, the same thing happened to me! Five casts, five sprints, and five fish is my limit too.

If the current is swift and the school obviously is moving with it, it pays to chase the wanderers by beach or boat. However, work the edges of any such schools and, if afloat, do not drive through the center. There is a special place across the River Styx made for boatmen who speed full throttle through the middle of surfaced bluefish. After my Navy days, I drew up blueprints for a small, but efficient, torpedo which could be launched by hand to speed such knuckleheads to their just reward. I never got it into production and sometimes regret my failure to do so.

One of the best visual signals to assist in spotting blues is bird action. During migration peaks of bluefish, I have seen gulls and terns working over stretches of water that cover miles. Frantic bait trying to escape the toothed predators under the surface fall easy prey to their aerial attackers.

Any feeding seabirds are worth investigating, but if blues are your target, watch the action of the birds carefully. If they dive under the water to pick up bait, it is almost a certainty that the fish driving that bait are not bluefish. Why this is true is simple to see when you look at the records of the stomach contents of bluefish examined by researchers. On many occasions, feathers, feet, and even bits of the body of gulls and terns have been discovered. Three times in my bluefishing life I have seen young terns disappear after having dived into a school of feeding blues. Once, I have seen a full grown herring gull, crippled so that it could not fly, torn to pieces by the fish. They are not gentle!

Following feeding birds is a common practice among boat anglers. In crowded waters, it can become a nuisance, for the entire fleet will head toward the commotion. One Montauk charter skipper I know —who shall remain nameless because he is still in business—has an excellent reputation among New York anglers as a bluefish guide. As a result, his every maneuver often is followed by many other boats when he attempts to zero in on feeding gulls and terns.

To lure the crowd elsewhere, he slyly drops a good supply of crumbled bread or crackers over the side. The birds scream and dive for the free meal, the fleet moves

This is good fly rod water, since it is sheltered from high winds.

Kip Bramhall, left, and the author casting with light tackle in a tidal estuary.

in, and the skipper quietly sails away to an area where competition is not so keen.

In clear water, blues often can be spotted even when they are not breaking the surface. Polarized glasses are extremely helpful in reducing the surface glare for such spotting. Learn to look through the water rather than at it. A good way to master this technique is to wade out waist deep and then examine your toes, booted or otherwise. You will soon be able to ignore the surface light and to distinguish submerged forms. Peering into the curl of a breaker is second nature to a surf fisherman. When dark, moving shadows are distinguished, the action starts.

In a feeding frenzy, blues will drive bait right onto the beach. Mangled and flopping small fish at the ocean's edge are a sure visual sign that bluefish are present. In the early winter of 1972, along the Outer Banks of North Carolina, locals took advantage of just such a phenomenon. Many of them dropped rods and reels, picked up gaffs, and waded into the blitz waters to take fish in quantity. This is hardly sporting, yet justifiable when a broiled fillet is at a premium. Some even grabbed the frenzied choppers with their bare hands, a practice I do not recommend if the grabber wants to keep all his fingerbones intact.

Height is a distinct advantage when trying to spot any fish underwater. The flying bridge or tuna tower on a boat gives the angler a much better picture of what goes on under the surface. From the beach, an overhanging bluff or sand dune performs the same service. Bobby Francis, guide and expert fisherman of Nantucket, at one time equipped his beach buggy with an aluminum ladder lashed to its rear. People laughed at him as he scaled this wobbly rig, but laughter changed to imitation when he located blues which others had passed by. Birds use altitude when searching for prey: anglers should do the same even when not airborne.

If you are fortunate enough to have a light plane at your disposal, bluefish may be distinguished rather easily from other schooling species. Do *not* look for a blue fish. Look instead for liquid shadows, normally darker than the bottom, which blend with the water surrounding them whether that water be blue, green, or a murky gray. Striped bass from the air have a brownish cast to their backs; channel bass are coppery; bonito and jacks are of a different shape than blues, as are most other semi-tropical species; weakfish are silvery. The late George Bonbright, who was a pioneer fly fisherman

A small portion of the party boat fleet drifting and chumming in the Acid Waters off the northern New Jersey coast. On some summer weekends there are nearly a thousand boats fishing this area.

in the oceans of the world, described bluefish as lying like huge, shadowy lead pencils when they could be seen through the surface glare. This is as good a description as any, and the color of the pencil adapts to the bottom over which it lies.

Color of the water itself is another visual indicator of where blues may, or may not, be. As a general rule, they do not like swimming in a muddy environment. The water need not necessarily be crystal clear, for much of the littoral ocean that is cloudy is rich in plankton, yet quantities of silt or sand in suspension will cause bluefish to move elsewhere. Oddly, this suspended material seems to bother large fish more than it does snappers. With their smaller gills, the youngsters should shun granules that might irritate membranes or even suffocate them, but such is not the case. I have taken snappers from roiled water that would cause any self-respecting adult to swim far away.

If a distinct line between two types of water can be seen, as is the case at the edge of the Gulf Stream or where a tidal river meets the sea, fish the clearer water. However, let the lure pass very close to the demarcation line, for plankton and bait are apt to be concentrated at that point. When afloat, the boat may well be in the cloudy section in order for the hooks to trail at this payoff edge.

Years ago, when the National Lead Company was ordered to stop polluting inshore waters with dilute sulfuric acid wastes, application was made to dump the material well offshore in the New York Bight area. Fishermen screamed to high heaven that it would ruin the fishing. Scientists of the Woods Hole Oceanographic Institution were brought into the fight by dumping proponents and stated that the dilute acid would produce almost harmless chemical salts the moment it hit the ocean. The scientists claimed the cloudy water resulting would vanish within a short time with a minimum of damage to the environment. National Lead and authorities in charge of issuing permits for offshore disposal took the researchers at their word and regular trips to sea by specially constructed barges commenced.

The famous "Acid Grounds" resulted. Charter, party, and private boats fish regularly in the wake of the barges that discharge the dilute sulfuric acid. For reasons which no one has been able to determine accurately, small bait apparently congregates at the edge of the discolored water—and bluefish congregate also. It is a classic case of mild pollution improving fishing. Obviously, this does not mean that ocean dumping is to be approved along all coasts, for parts of the New York Bight have become a dead sea of sorts due to indescriminate disposal of all types of refuse. However, the "Acid Grounds" are one exception.

Salinity should also be considered when seeking out good bluefishing waters. Rarely, if ever, will blues venture into purely fresh coastal rivers. They will chase bait schools into a tidal estuary that is brackish, but when all salt is missing, they turn tail even if the foraging is good. As is true in the case of murky water, the smaller specimens apparently can stand extremes better than their parents. Snappers, therefore, will be found farther up current than adults. Anglers are not in the habit of carrying salinometers in their tackle boxes. A simple taste test will serve the purpose. If there is no salty tang on the tongue, look elsewhere for blues.

In the vast majority of cases, the bluefisherman will be faced with a wide expanse of ocean, no birds screaming and dipping, no fish in sight, in fact no indication whatsoever that the sea is anything other than a biological desert. What then?

Look for a clash of currents. Such spots may be in many forms, such as tide rips, river water meeting the ocean, or turbulence over a reef or bar. They may extend for miles, as is true of The Race at the eastern end of Long Island Sound off the Connecticut shore, or may be only a few feet in diameter as in the case of a current eddy swirling behind a rock. Although bluefish may pass through water which is undisturbed by backwashes and swirls, usually they are transients only through such areas. Where the currents meet, they tend to lie for long periods, often many hours.

The reason for this is simple. Take a fish—any fish. Note that its back normally is of a much darker shade than its belly. If an individual fish were subjected to the same amount of light on both back and belly, there would be no demarcation line, something proved by scientists who have provided such unnatural conditions in an aquarium. However, nature probably planned the dark back and light underside so that predators from above would have difficulty spotting their meal against the comparatively dark ocean floor or water depths, while predators from below would have similar trouble outlining their quarry against a lighter sky. Tip that same fish on its side or back and it becomes highly visible.

Visibility may be only momentary as a bait fish is tumbled, out of control, in a current, but a hungry bluefish lurking down current needs only a moment to zero in on its target. Even such natural foods as squid, which does not have sharply contrasting colors on back and belly, can be seen more readily when flipped tentacles-over-eyes by an unexpected water force. Like a teenager falling downstairs, the bait becomes all arms and legs. Undoubtedly, also like a teenager, squid and other baits give off sounds of alarm under such circumstances, and the predator reacts.

Even in a flat calm, ocean waters are never still. The rotation of the earth sets up currents, effects of which are felt all over the world. Tides, produced basically

by the gravitational pull of the moon and sun, add to this motion. The geographical configuration of both land masses and the ocean floor influence currents locally. Add winds, fresh-water run-off from the polar ice caps and rainfall, man-made structures in and over the water, and the equation becomes highly complex.

Nothing can beat local knowledge when it comes to determining the places and times of current clashes, where bluefish will be found. However, a stranger can prepare himself in advance so that his chances of success are improved. The first thing to remember is that the time of tide change is not necessarily the time of current change. For example, the flood tide current off Point Judith, Rhode Island, starts to move in a westerly direction approximately three hours before the actual time of low tide at that point.

Locals may memorize such specific bits of information, but those who wish to do some pioneering on their own should invest in the excellent *Tide Tables* and *Current Tables* published by the National Ocean Survey—a part of the National Oceanic and Atmospheric Administration under the United States Department of Commerce. These are available not only from regional headquarters of the Survey, but also from a host of private agencies along all coasts. Most major marine equipment dealers handle the publications, as well as nautical charts.

Charts themselves are vital to any angler who has more than a passing interest in bluefishing, or any other kind of fishing for that matter. Water depths, configuration of the land, location of navigational aids, type of bottom, major tide rips, and many other factors important to success are indicated. Detail depends upon the scale of charts purchased. The more de-

Furious surf at Great Point Rip, Nantucket.

tail, the better, so the few extra dollars invested in additional charts will pay off in fish caught.

Armed with charts and current and tide tables, the angler can do a good deal of homework prior to setting out in order to locate the best potential grounds. Equally important, he can determine in general the best times of day for fishing. Although on rare occasions I have taken blues when current or tide was slack, preferred conditions are when the water is moving swiftly. If a moderate wind is blowing against the flow of current, conditions may be considered ideal.

To generalize is dangerous, but I plan to do it anyway. In most areas, the two hours before and after the time of high tide—omitting the period of slack water—are usually most productive. As far as currents are concerned, the last hour of the current run in any given direction normally brings the best fishing.

There are obvious exceptions to these generalities. At the mouth of a tidal river or estuary, bait works into the shallows as the tide rises and flats are covered. Although small blues may follow the feed, larger specimens tend to wait until the tide starts to ebb and food is washed seaward. As the shallows are bared, minnows and the like are forced into the deeper channels and are carried by the current against their will to the open ocean. Lurking near the bars off the mouth, blues lie in wait to feast upon out-of-control smaller creatures. Under such conditions, the general rule concerning the last hour of the outgoing current holds, but that concerning high tide does not. The first hour of the incoming current may be worthless due to the lack of water depth, so this generality is also torpedoed.

Neophytes often have difficulty in believing that a current or tide change can make a tremendous difference when bluefishing. This was brought home to me while acting as "professor" at the special short course on marine sport fishing conducted annually under the sponsorship of North Carolina State University. The students, for the most part, are angling beginners of all ages. The group had embarked in various boats and all were trolling for small blues in the vicinity of Hatteras Inlet. Birds and fish were everywhere, excitement ran high, and I was spending a high proportion of my time untangling lines, advising all and sundry how to hook fish and not each other, and generally acting as a much-too-talkative mate.

Within a matter of minutes, the tremendously fast fishing came to a screeching halt. Terns and gulls flew quietly to land to preen themselves and digest their meals. The bluefish literally seemed to disappear. Students looked around in dismay and obviously decided that some underwater calamity had taken place. In point of fact, the current had slacked and the fishing, as it turned out, was finished for the day. This made a good subject for my spontaneous lecture to the captive audience in the cockpit on the effects of current on bluefish feeding habits, but I have a strong feeling that the students would have preferred more fish!

When currents are strong, rips may be located without too much trouble. Even when no winds blow, the water surface is rippled and remains so over a long period of time. Permanent rips are those which appear regularly, day after day, month after month, in approximately the same geographical position. Many, as noted above, are plotted on navigational charts.

Temporary rips are different. They may appear on one tide phase and vanish on another, be present when the wind blows from the northwest and disappear when it blows from the southeast. The configuration of the land and also of the ocean floor will influence these temporary rips considerably. Along sandy beaches, un-

Claude Rogers leans into a hooked bluefish off the Virginia Capes.

fortunately for the angler, these temporary rips may change their location after every major storm as the sand itself is shifted by water action.

The study of charts may be of some help, but study on the scene by means of a fathometer is more practical in such cases. Where there is a sharp drop-off, chances are good that there will be a current clash of some sort at some particular change of tide. Note the location, fix the boat's position by observation of navigational aids or shore markers, then mark the spot on your chart. Return to that spot when the currents change and you may well be successful.

The surf fisherman has no fathometer at his disposal, yet he can also spot such areas. My own procedure when fishing strange beaches is to visit the area at dead low tide. Then offshore bars, sloughs— which are channels running parallel to the beach between it and an offshore bar —cuts in the bars, holes, and underwater obstructions are revealed. By making a mental note of the best locations and, if necessary, by arranging driftwood or rocks to mark the key points, it is not difficult to return to payoff water when the tide is more favorable.

As is true in the case of tidal rivers and estuaries, bait fish will come into a slough through a cut in the offshore bar as the water rises. When the water falls again, bait will be washed to sea through the same cut. As a general rule, fish the inshore side of such cuts on the rising tide, the offshore side on the falling. Even when the bars are entirely covered, both bait and bluefish congregate at these points.

Although they can hardly be glorified by the name of rips, those spots on the downcurrent side of underwater obstruc-

tions often hold bluefish just as similar lies in fresh water hold trout. Again, bait is tumbled about as the current carries it by and the predator has easy pickings. Pinpoint casting from a small boat or from the beach soon separates the amateur from the experienced angler under such conditions.

This holds true in the case of manmade obstructions as I found to my chagrin while pier fishing at Venice, Florida. The beach there is relatively unbroken in contour and the pier is therefore popular. One old timer, whose name I never learned, had staked out a claim on the downcurrent side of a particular piling. Almost toothless, he was sucking on an unlighted cigar, which grew smaller and smaller as time passed and as he derricked up bluefish after bluefish from a point almost under his feet. The blues were small, but they were a lot larger than the nothings I caught as I—and several others—danced around him in an attempt to reach the magic few feet of productive water.

Finally, I stopped fishing and engaged the ancient in conversation. My Yankee

These young anglers are after snapper bluefish from a footbridge over a tidal stream.

accent seemed to fascinate him and he confided that he had fished that particular pier regularly ever since it had been built. After much observation and experimentation, he had discovered that many species, but bluefish in particular, hung around that particular piling at half tide. Obviously the bait supply and water conditions were ideal at that time.

While on the Florida scene, I should mention that adult bluefish in that state normally move into far more shallow water than they do along the northern Atlantic coast. Rips and inlets there are prime producers, yet the fish will be found in Florida areas that might be considered snapper waters to the north. The explana-

tion for this behavior is simple: blues are slaves to their stomachs. On the long, sandy beaches, foraging is poor unless bait can be herded into the shallows. Inlets, piers, and bridges of course produce the current clashes I keep emphasizing, but elsewhere the fish will feed on targets of opportunity and will even risk stranding as they pursue fleeing mullet.

Leaving currents and rips, let me look at the bottom of the sea for a moment. Fishermen often ask me whether or not bluefish prefer sandy, rocky, muddy, or shell bottoms as their swimming grounds. There is no pat answer. I have caught them over the pure sands of Nantucket beaches, the tumbled rock and clay off

Gay Head on Martha's Vineyard, the "pluff mud," as the natives call the soft stuff in the channels of South Carolina's Cape Romain, and the oyster shells that pave parts of Chesapeake Bay. They feed where the food is found. If I were to say the type of bottom which blues seem to prefer when there is a choice, I would opt for something other than mud. If there is no choice, disregard this advice.

Wind, on the other hand, can have a major effect on bluefishing. In a flat calm, blues may feed and may be caught, but it is more difficult to persuade them to hit a lure or bait than when the ocean's surface is ruffled. Undoubtedly this is because they have a better look at the offering and can see that something is wrong with it. Active surf along a beach will bring blues in close, yet too much surf will roil the water and drive the quarry offshore. As previously noted, wind working against a current results in prime bluefishing conditions.

The direction of the wind also influences catches. Unfortunately, what is a good wind for one area often is a bad one for another. Years ago, I mentioned to Morrie Upperman, angler and lure maker of Atlantic City, New Jersey, that the dying away of a northerly storm meant top bluefishing in the Cape Cod area. He looked at me as though I had rocks in my head. On his own home grounds near Barnegat Bay, such conditions ruin the fishing! For a visiting angler, the best bet is to inquire locally to determine just what breeze direction is considered ideal and to make a mental or actual note of it.

Only one rule can be applied almost universally: for the surf angler, wind in his face will produce better results than wind at his back over the long haul. The reason for this is obvious—bait is driven close to the beach and the predatory bluefish follow it.

To describe every feature of good bluefishing water is almost impossible. A barren area may be transformed into an angler's heaven in a matter of moments if wind, tide, water, and bait cooperate properly. If there is only one general condition to avoid, I would classify dirty or extremely roiled water as this condition. There is even an exception here. When the sea is filled with a light, line-clogging weed known as goglum, blues seem to thrive in it. Water between the tiny weed patches is clear, but to move a line through the area is to dredge up pounds of the floating organisms. Lures that weigh a few ounces soon weigh pounds after a few feet of travel and their effectiveness is destroyed. Bluefish like goglum: I disagree with them.

Over a period of nearly 300 years, some bluefishing waters have stood the test of time. When the fish are on a down cycle of plenty, they will still be caught in reduced numbers on these grounds and, when the cycle swings upward, they will return in numbers there before appearing elsewhere. In what follows, I have made no attempt to pinpoint exact locations, for this would be impossible due to the shifting currents, bars, and beaches. The general areas, however, will indicate where an angler has the best possible chance of taking adult bluefish. Note the qualifying "adult." Snapper grounds change so often that it is fruitless to mention them. A hot spot this year may be cold as ice in twelve months.

North of Boston, Massachusetts, good bluefishing is rare except during the years of a true glut. At such times, blues are basically targets of opportunity, found while after other species such as striped bass. Waters in which the two species are found often have similar characteristics. I might add that, contrary to the belief of some, bluefish usually do not drive stripers away. Because they are quicker than the bass, they may hit the lure first, yet the two species may be found time and time again feeding together in a rip. Large

Bluefish and striped bass, both caught in the same waters. Although blues can beat bass to a lure, they do not necessarily drive the stripers from a fishing area.

bluefish may chomp on small stripers—and *vice versa*—in special circumstances, yet the two do not bother each other extensively when the target is a third party.

Although some small fish may be found during a normal year along the coastline between Cohasset and Plymouth, the best bet is Cape Cod Bay, thence around the tip of the Cape at Provincetown southward to the Cape's spur at Monomoy Point. From Monomoy to Great Point on Nantucket Island, there is a series of tide rips which form one of the best bluefishing grounds in the Northeast.

Nantucket itself, with its neighboring small islands of Tuckernuck and Muskeget, has been prime bluefish water since Colonial times. If there are any blues at all to be found in Massachusetts when the cycle is on the downswing, Nantucket is the place to find them. The season runs from early June right through October and even into November when the autumn is mild.

Nantucket Sound—bounded by Nantucket itself, Martha's Vineyard, and the southern shore of Cape Cod—is all good water. Oddly enough, the fish appear to arrive along the southeastern shore of the Cape even before they are taken on the islands. This may be because anglers fish for them there specifically, while the islanders in late May are preoccupied with striped bass.

From the Vineyard, which provides good fishing from both beach and boat, westward throughout Vineyard Sound, along the Elizabeth Islands, and in Buzzards Bay, bluefishing can be considered a way of life for many. Several years ago, I would have written that the blues were long gone by the end of October, but in 1972 a group jigging for cod off Gay Head on Martha's Vineyard discovered blues feeding on the bottom and did well. The date was mid-November, which indicates to me that fishing deep might well get results in many other spots in this area.

The connection between Cape Cod Bay and Buzzards Bay is one of many monuments to engineering knowledge found along the coasts. The Cape Cod Canal and other similar canals were all designed to permit passage of ships from one point to another without the risk of steaming through dangerous offshore waters. A side effect in such constructions has been man-made bluefishing grounds. Currents are swift, bait fish have a worrisome existence, and hungry blues take advantage of the fact. Do not neglect canals even when they are small in size. They have the advantage of being fishable when high winds make other areas untenable for the angler.

Moving down the coast, Nomans Land, mentioned earlier as a bluefish spawning area, is at the eastern border of Rhode Island Sound. Block Island is on the western edge of Rhode Island Sound and is sur-

Cort Naegelin unhooks a blue taken off Horseshoe Shoals, Cape Cod.

Bluefishing in the surf at Wasque Point, Martha's Vineyard.

The author casting into the surf at Wasque Point.

rounded by excellent fishing water, complete with rips, bars, beaches, and rocky shallows. The water itself is exceptionally clear and on the average is considerably cooler than the ocean to the north and east. For this reason, blues normally arrive a bit later than they do off southern Cape Cod, yet the migrations in the autumn will extend into November.

Along the Rhode Island mainland, the various points are favored by both surf fishermen and boatmen. Watch Hill Point, Weekapaug Point, Point Judith, Brenton Point and the reef near it, Sakonnet Point, and Beavertail Point are among the best known. On the Massachusetts islands, waters connecting tidal ponds with

the sea are known as openings. In Rhode Island, they are called breachways. All of them, particularly on the outgoing tide, furnish excellent bluefishing. If you hear a Rhode Islander state that they are murdering them at Charlestown or Quonny Breachway, do not think he is talking about a military action. Incidentally, when you look for Quonny on the chart, try Quonochontaug instead. Only the Indians give it its full name today.

In Colonial times, all of Narragansett Bay, even as far north as Providence, where the water salinity drops, was good fishing water. With the arrival of the blessings of modern civilization, much of the area became so badly polluted that bluefish swam elsewhere. Fortunately, the trend has been reversed and, as the Bay became cleaner, the fish returned. Although big choppers rarely appear in the upper reaches of the Bay, there is good bluefishing throughout the area. Because of private ownership and difficulties in reaching the shore overland, this section is best tackled via a small boat.

Block Island Sound is a sort of aquatic stopper at the entrance to Long Island Sound. Rips are plentiful, and so are the bluefish. It is not water for a small outboard skiff, although many simpletons take their lives in their hands in such craft. All too often, they lose their grip, and the Coast Guard statistics grimly prove it.

Between Fishers Island and Little Gull Island lies The Race, which undoubtedly is the best known bluefishing area off the Connecticut shore. Here, depths exceed more than 200 feet and the water is seldom still. Blues congregate in the many rips and may be taken from the surface right down to the bottom. It pays to experiment by fishing at many levels until the payoff depth is hit. Again, a seaworthy boat is recommended, for seas can build up in a very short time when the current turns against the wind.

Elsewhere along the Connecticut coast, the best bluefishing lies from Sachem Head easterly to the Rhode Island border. When the cycles of plenty are on the upswing, as they were in the early 1970's, fish will venture much farther west, but this cannot be depended upon in what is called a normal year. The Falkner Island area south of Guilford; Six Mile Reef off Clinton; the Bloody Grounds, lying south of the Connecticut River mouth and northwest of Plum Island; and The Gut, labelled Plum Gut on the charts, between Plum Island and Orient Point on Long Island, are among the best-known grounds.

Although trolling and chumming were once the basic methods used by anglers in the Nutmeg State, more and more of them are turning to light tackle casting, both from boats and from shore. Since the coast is dotted with islands, rocks, and tidal streams of all sizes, it is ideal for this type of fishing. Each season turns up new hot spots as fishermen of imagination continue to explore.

On the New York side of Long Island Sound, bluefish for reasons best known to themselves are not as plentiful as they are on the Connecticut side. The exception is the Montauk Point area, which technically delineates the limits of Block Island Sound rather than Long Island Sound. Shagwong Reef and Cerberus Shoal are prime areas, yet the whole Montauk section, complete with tide rips both inshore and offshore, produces well from both beach and boat. Perhaps more than anywhere else in the northeast, catches are affected by water temperatures. Montaukers may complain about bluefish scarcity at times when fish are being slaughtered to the east, west, and north of them. Almost without exception, the cause can be found with a thermometer. Eddies of cold water may lie for days and even weeks at a time off the Point, and these eddies act as an effective barrier to cruising blues.

The south, or ocean, shore of New York's Long Island has its best fishing both from beach and boat at or near the main inlets—Rockaway, Jones, Fire Island, Moriches, and Shinnecock. This is logical, for concentrations of bait swept out of the bays are far greater than along open expanses of sandy beach. As is true in the Montauk area, the fish often will remain into late November unless a cold northeaster sends them scurrying to warmer climes.

Although water pollution problems have hexed some bluefishing on the northern shore of Long Island, the species has been taken in recent years more commonly than since the early 1800's. The whole Gardiner's Bay area at the entrance to the Sound produces good catches, but success tapers off as the angler works west. Bluefish Shoal off Port Chester was not named for weakfish! However, except in years of glut, chances of hooking big blues off Lloyd Point and Eaton's Neck, where they once were plentiful, are slim. If the pollution is cleaned up, these grounds may come into their own again.

Pollution is also a problem throughout the Hudson River Gorge, which runs something west of south out of New York Harbor to the edge of the Continental Shelf. In one portion of the New York Bight, where ocean dumping has been going on for many years, the bottom has been made a biological desert. Those bluefish caught in the area usually are sorry specimens indeed, with fin rot and other diseases evident. However, if present restrictions on dumping are enforced, chances are good that the entire area once again will yield giant blues as it did years ago.

Gluttony brings the blues to the dirty rips and currents that surge around Sandy Hook, New Jersey. The area teems with bait of all kinds and the choppers figuratively hold their noses and move in. From the Hook to Cape May, Jersey has long been famed as a bluefishing area, and with good reason. South of Long Beach Island, the major runs are in the spring and fall with a few small specimens available all summer. North of that same island, there are many summer residents augmented at each end of the fishing season by the migrants from other areas.

Off northern New Jersey, an incredible fleet of boats—party, charter, and private —gathers each season to ladle ground menhaden as chum into the water on an around-the-clock basis. No one has calculated either the tonnage of chum or of bluefish caught by this operation. However, gourmets claim that blues taken once the season is in full swing in the area taste more of mossbunker than they do of bluefish! True or not, catches border on the incredible, and anglers of all ages, shapes, and sizes happily lug them home to a waiting skillet.

The offshore chumming fleet is not the only taker of blues along the Jersey shore. Despite many claims from other areas, I believe there is no question that surf casting with an artificial lure, using a rod and free-spool reel, originated in New Jersey, and the basic quarry was bluefish. Casting a metal lure, or "squid," gave rise to the term "squidding," which is applied today in many areas to all artificial-lure surf fishing with conventional tackle.

I am not about to antagonize chambers of commerce along the Jersey coast by recommending one surf fishing or light tackle casting area over another. Suffice it to say that blues are found all along this shoreline during the seasons noted above. As elsewhere, the inlets—Shark River, Sea Girt, Manasquan, Barnegat, Beach Haven, Brigantine, Absecon, Great Egg Harbor, Corson, and Townsend—provide prime angling. Access is sometimes a problem, but even among the crowded bikinis of Atlantic City fish may be taken. Small blues work up into the bays and sounds lying behind the barrier beach and, unless heavy rainfall brings too much fresh water run-off, light tackle buffs can do well.

For boat fishermen, the best-known areas are the Acid Grounds and the general Sandy Hook section; Shrewsbury Rocks off Seabright; the Ridges off Manasquan; and the waters off both Beach Haven and Barnegat Inlets. These are better known than similar waters to the south simply because the season runs from June through November—always providing the weather behaves. In the late 1960's and early 1970's, bluefish appeared in considerable quantity in the Cape May area and, hopefully, will continue to do so for some years to come. Prior to that time, all except the smaller specimens had apparently bypassed much of Cape May for a decade or more.

Delaware's short Atlantic coastline from the Maryland border to Cape Henlopen has spring and fall fishing. This section is one of the very few where the spring run is heavier than the autumn one. The Hump, off Indian River Inlet, is the best known offshore spot, lying about 15 miles out to sea. For the beach fisherman, Rehoboth and Bethany Beaches, plus the area around Indian River Inlet, produce well.

Due to heavy pollution, blues shunned Delaware Bay for many decades. Fortunately, this fouling is on the wane and there is now sport for small-boat operators as far north as Bombay Hook. Most catches are of specimens under five pounds. Even in Colonial days, it is doubtful that bluefish ever were abundant much farther north than Reedy Point due to low water salinity.

Roughly seven miles off the Atlantic coast of Maryland there is an area which approximately parallels the coastal contour from Isle of Wight Shoal to Great Gull Bank that produces big bluefish

A bluefish is brought alongside a boat fishing off the Virginia Capes.

A charter boat heads home after a day's fishing off the Virginia Capes.

from late May into July and again from about mid-September through November. Oddly, smaller blues hang around Isle of Wight Shoal and Fenwick Shoal to the north even during the summer months. Maryland watermen have a descriptive name for small shoals—they call them lumps—and First Lump, west of Little Gull Bank, is a good trolling and chumming spot in spring and fall. Southwest and Southeast Lumps, roughly eight miles to the south, yield bluefish all summer long. The Jack Spot, famous for white marlin, also produces in spring and fall, much to the annoyance of skippers who have spent hours rigging baits for billfish.

Inshore, there is bluefishing along all of the Maryland Atlantic shore, with emphasis on the spring and fall runs for surf and small-boat anglers. Small fish even work up into Isle of Wight Bay. I will come to the Chesapeake Bay side in a moment.

The northern end of Assateague Island is the best bet for the surf fisherman who wants bluefish. To the south and west, across the Virginia border, the island is channel bass water. Offshore, the Sugar Lumps and Winter Quarter Shoal are prime grounds and Blackfish Bank yields big fish in the late fall. As is true off Maryland, the many shoals that parallel the whole Virginia coast well offshore are good trolling grounds. To name them all would be to catalog the offshore waters.

Cape Charles and Cape Henry form the entrance to Chesapeake Bay. In former times, anglers concentrated their bluefishing efforts around Cape Charles in spring and fall, but the fishing has now been opened up around Cape Henry. The spring run is good, yet passes by rather rapidly. From late October into January, weather permitting, the area from the Bay Bridge-Tunnel complex right into the open ocean produces spectacular fishing for what are called jumbos by Virginians. Mankind rarely improves salt water fishing by his construction efforts, but the Bay Bridge-Tunnel is a happy exception to the rule.

Moving up Chesapeake Bay along both the Virginia and Maryland shores, the size of individual bluefish diminishes the farther one gets from the ocean. William C. Schroeder, author of *Fishes of Chesapeake Bay,* reports that straggling bluefish appear in late March in Bay waters. In my opinion, some may even winter over in lower Chesapeake areas during a mild winter. Although a few are taken around Swan Point Channel, the Bay just north of Annapolis Bridge may be considered their northern limit in the Bay for all practical angling purposes.

With dozens of bait-filled rivers flowing into salt water, with hundreds of channels and inlets, with tidal conditions that may change at any time because of steady winds, with salinities varying greatly after a heavy rainfall, it is not extraordinary that bluefishing in Chesapeake Bay is not confined to a single spot. Among the better known areas are: Winter and Summer Gooses off the Choptank River mouth; the Hooper Island area; Northwest and Southwest Middle Grounds; the Windmill Point area, and Bluefish Rock off the mouth of the Back River. However, what is a good spot today may draw a blank tomorrow with a shift of wind. Local boat captains and newspaper rod and gun writers keep a close eye on movements of the schools and it is well to follow their advice.

Although trolling has long been the favorite method of taking bluefish in the Chesapeake Bay area, more and more anglers are discovering that casting, particularly to surfaced fish, works well from both beach and boat. If in the latter, keep a close eye on the weather, for sudden squalls can turn the Bay from a serene, huge millpond into a very dangerous stretch of water indeed. I learned this to my cost many years ago when a boat from

Bob Hutchinson, outdoor editor for the Norfolk Virginian-Pilot, *hefts a bluefish taken off Virginia Beach.*

Cape Point at Hatteras, North Carolina, during a bluefish blitz.

which I was fishing south of Mobjack Bay swamped due to my own stupidity.

Returning to the ocean side once again, bluefish migrations cut in closer to shore from Cape Henry to the North Carolina line than they do in many areas. Therefore, it pays to work the beach and the area out to about five miles along Virginia Beach and the Sandbridge section. The area four miles east of Sandbridge and the Tiger Wreck Lumps, another five miles east, are particular hot spots. From the Virginia-North Carolina line to a point a scant two miles off Corolla, there is a similar stretch where big bluefish congregate during November and December. Undoubtedly they are there

also in the spring, but few boats work the area at that time.

Surf fishing along the outer beaches of North Carolina is good for bluefish in spring and late fall when the larger fish sag inshore. Unfortunately, they do this all too seldom, but snappers and blues slightly larger can be taken almost all year. As the Outer Banks area becomes more easily distinguished by its seaward barrier benches—in general, the beaches from Duck Woods to Hatteras—fishing improves. Large fish in early spring and late fall, often into the winter months, appear from the beach right out to the western edge of the Gulf Stream.

For boatmen, normally the best area for

big choppers is about halfway between the shore and the Stream. Surf, pier, and small-boat anglers must hope for bait close in; otherwise, they must settle for smaller fish. However, these smaller specimens may be taken throughout most of the summer. They stick fairly close to shore and work up into the many sounds in the area also.

Oregon Inlet, which separates Nags Head from Hatteras Island, is the first major break in the beach front working southward from the Virginia line. Famed for fishing over the years, it has become even more popular since the establishment of the Cape Hatteras National Seashore. My first trip across the inlet many years ago was via an antiquated ferry which ran when the skipper saw fit, carried two cars at most, and deposited those willing to make the trip on a sand track that ran along the beach. Often, I might add, the skipper did not see fit. Today, there is a paved highway across the bridge spanning the water, and this highway runs inside the dunes along all of Hatteras Island itself.

Hatteras blues, the name given years ago to specimens in that area between five and eight pounds, have now grown even larger, up to and including the 31-pound, 12-ounce monster taken on January 30, 1972, that I mentioned earlier. The fact that this catch was made at Hatteras Inlet between Hatteras and Ocracoke Islands shows that large blues sag inshore from time to time. These slammers, however, are where you find them due not only to the vagaries of the Gulf Stream offshore, but also to the bait supply carried by winds and currents which may change drastically from day to day along all of the Outer Banks.

At the time it was caught, James Hussey's all-tackle record fish was unusual in that it was hooked very late in the season. In previous years, the end of December spelled finish to bluefishing. However,

winter fishing in recent years off the general Hatteras area has become common. Water temperatures have remained high, undoubtedly due to variations in the Gulf Stream, and the bluefish have remained close enough to shore to provide excellent sport for surf-casters.

Obviously no one can state definitely that this warming trend will last over a long period. It does, however, present a good argument in favor of the fact that blues move offshore to some extent during the winter rather than move to the south in a body. Given warm water, they simply stay where the feed is plentiful. If the water happens to be warm at the surf line, they will be there.

Miles of white sand beach extend along this shore of North Carolina. Surf fishermen look for breaks in the outer bars. Boatmen cruise around the dangerous waters between Diamond Shoals and the Gulf Stream. Small craft operators and waders cover the eastern part of Pamlico Sound. All of them take bluefish. Note also that big blues remain on the ocean side of this area throughout the winter, and blitz fishing can happen along any part of the beach when weather conditions make angling possible. Because Cape Hatteras is the dividing point between semitropical and temperate waters on the eastern seaboard, temperature clashes of air and water often result in storms that make angling anything but possible.

The coastline cuts sharply westward south of the Cape and, although there is good bluefishing at times along the Ocracoke and Portsmouth Island beaches, chances are that the fisherman will have to go further offshore to get into big fish.

The Core Banks and Cape Lookout National Seashore take over after leaving Portsmouth Island. This huge stretch of beach, extending to Cape Lookout itself, is lightly fished when compared to the Nags

Head-Hatteras area. The various small inlets are the best bet. Offshore boat fishing is not common simply because good harbors are not within easy running distance until the Cape Lookout area is reached. Here, Cape Lookout Shoals produce the biggest fish for boatmen while shore-based anglers and small-boat buffs take smaller specimens along Shackleford Banks to the north and west.

From Beaufort Inlet west along the Bogue Banks, thence southwest and south to Cape Fear and Frying Pan Shoals, the picture is similar. Small bluefish are taken from beach, boat, and pier, particularly at the inlets—of which there are dozens—from April through November. Undoubtedly, if anglers were to brave the elements in the dead of winter, they would have success. Offshore craft based at Southport have picked up some jumbo blues in recent years around Frying Pan Shoals and to the southeast of that area.

Since migrations move along this section, there is a good chance of future development of this fishery even though it is a long haul to the edge of the Gulf Stream.

I should note that boatmen heading for offshore waters along all of North Carolina's southwest coast undoubtedly would catch large blues if they fished for them. However, usually they are heading to sea at high speed to reach grounds where big game fish, king mackerel, and other species may be caught readily and, logically, do not want to expend gasoline and time searching. In addition, the season for taking passing blues is earlier than that for other offshore species in the spring, and later in the autumn.

West of Cape Fear to the South Carolina line, again the picture is similar. Lockwood's Folly Inlet—a name that has always intrigued me—Shallotte, and Tubbs Inlet are the best areas. Fishing piers stud this part of the coast and many bluefish

Joel Arrington adds another bluefish to his collection while fishing on the Outer Banks of North Carolina.

are taken from them from April right through November.

A quick glance at a chart of the South Carolina coast shows immediately that its character is quite different from that of its neighbor to the northeast. Although there are some long expanses of sand, such as that at Myrtle Beach, there is no overall barrier stretching for miles with sounds lying behind it. The coast becomes more tropical in nature with hundreds of small islands, tidal rivers and streams, and flat tracts of marshland extending over acres of creeks and shallows. Nutrients in these marshes make this an important nursery ground for all sorts of game and bait fishes. Unfortunately, these same characteristics do not make inshore waters the best for bluefish. Fresh water run-off tends to muddy the creeks and estuaries, and bluefish are not crazy about roiled water. Therefore, look for South Carolina blues seaward of the marshes primarily.

From the North Carolina border to Murrell's Inlet, beach, pier, and small-boat fishing all get results throughout a good part of the year. Blues range in size from snappers up to about eight pounds, with a five pounder considered a good one. Working south and west, the area around North and South Islands is favored. The outer islands around Cape Romain, thence south to Charleston, furnish similar fishing. Offshore angling by larger craft seeking big game out of Charleston recently has been developed. It is a long haul from that part of the coast to the Gulf Stream, but my educated guess is that more and more really big blues will be taken as this angling effort develops further.

The sections around Charleston, Beaufort, and Hilton Head are all expanding rapidly as resorts. With the subsequent increase in angling populations, there is no question that new grounds will be opened up. It appears that late fall is the best time

to make such an effort.

If you plan light-tackle casting from any of the sod banks or marsh areas along the South Carolina coast, watch your footing carefully. I once vaulted neatly over the bow of a Boston Whaler near Cape Romain while out with Buddy Bennett and Jack Mitchell of Charleston and sank almost instantly to my waist in "pluff mud." Extracting me from this gummy substance was a major effort, and I learned the hard way to walk where running water could be seen and where the bottom was firm.

The southern coast of South Carolina and that of Georgia are very similar in character and in bluefish possibilities. The series of islands, tidal streams, and estuaries from Savannah to Cumberland Island mean murky water inshore along most of Georgia's coast. Snappers and some slightly larger fish are taken from shore and pier as well as from small boats, but catches for the most part are incidental to those made when after other species. The Savannah area; Sapelo Island in McIntosh County; Sea, St. Simons, and Jekyll Islands near Brunswick; and Cumberland Island itself are the best known spots. As in South Carolina, this is because these sections are well-known resorts. Best fishing is offshore where the effects of fresh water run-off are diminished.

The coastline bends westward after crossing into Florida and, once again, its character changes, with true barrier beaches separating bays from the Atlantic Ocean. The water is clear for the most part and blues are found all along the east coast. Seasonal runs of fish up to about five pounds start in late September in northern Florida and are first taken from piers, beaches, and small boats. As winter progresses, the fish move into the bays. There is another run in the spring, although a few blues are taken all through the year after the majority have swum northward. It would be impossible to list all areas where blues are caught, but I will try to hit the high spots.

From Fernandina Beach to Cape Kennedy, very few jumbo bluefish are taken during the course of the year. Their smaller brethren concentrate around the inlets as they move inshore, yet action can be fast from piers and beaches when feeding blues chase bait right up to the shoreline. This same type of action is common at Cocoa and usually is sparked by a northeast blow.

A stretch from the Jensen Beach bridge south for about five miles is a particularly hot area for shore casters. The Crossroads, an area at the junction of Indian River—actually, a lagoon—and the St. Lucie River, is an excellent fishing ground from October through March. Ernie Lyons, the sage of Stuart, drew my attention to a small group of secretive anglers in that part of the world who have discovered several spots which produce extraordinarily large bluefish equal in weight to those found almost anywhere along the coast. When the sun is high, such catches are rare, but at dusk, dawn, and the night hours, results can be startling on these winter-overing fish.

The inlets around Salerno, Juno, and Riviera Beaches are other sections where a northeast wind brings the blues close to shore. As is true elsewhere, inlets are the best bets.

When you reach Lake Worth waters at Palm Beach, you have hit the best bluefishing in Florida. Tony Accetta, founder of the lure company that bears his name, used to try new designs on both large and small blues here and would discard those that did poorly. By fishing many lines at one time, he could get an excellent comparative picture among the various lures used.

Commercial fishermen exploit this fishing by trolling deep with hook and line, particularly in the vicinity of Peanut Island, and sportsmen have followed their lead. Night fishing on the full moon is considered optimum, yet blues of all sizes, from snappers to those pressing twenty pounds, are taken even during daylight. Casting also should not be neglected.

The inlet area at Boynton Beach has long been famous for runs of huge jack crevalle. When they come inshore, bluefish often are mingled with them. Bait fish suffer—anglers do not. From this point down through Miami to Cape Florida Light, there is also some inshore fishing for small blues. However, along the Florida Keys, bluefish must be considered a minor species and catches are incidental when after other game.

Rounding the tip of Florida to the Gulf of Mexico, bluefish up to about four pounds are taken in November and December, then again in March, from East Cape to Naples. Between Naples and Clearwater, the season peaks a bit earlier during both the late fall and early spring runs.

Inshore, throughout most of Florida's Gulf of Mexico side, and often on the close-in offshore waters, bluefish arrive in the spring—usually in late March or early April. As the season progresses, they school along the coasts of Alabama, Mississippi, Louisiana, and the northern coast of Texas. Fresh water run-off from the river systems, however, may drive them away from the beach areas.

These fish rarely attain the size of those found along the Atlantic coast. A good one would be a five or six pounder. Taken by both shore casters and boatmen, they are often found in the same areas as Spanish mackerel.

Gulf blues are not a separate species, although all of those beached or boated in semitropical waters are lighter in color than their counterparts in the cold north. This may be a normal change of coloration due to environment—a common thing among many fish. The northern seas are gray-green while those of the Gulf salt water are powder-blue. The fish are simply adapting their own camouflage to their surroundings.

Earlier in this book, I have listed the general world-wide range of bluefish and have highlighted some of the better spots outside the United States. It is not my intention to give a port-by-port rundown of foreign fishing areas primarily because good information is scanty in many sections. Secondarily, I think it unlikely that the inhabitants of Morocco or of Istanbul will stampede in their rush to the bookstores to see whether or not I have included their favorite fishing grounds. For those who wish to try their bluefishing luck outside of the United States, study the first part of this chapter, and make friends with the necessary foreigners.

Good bluefishing water is much the same the world over. The trick is to recognize it.

Bluefish can be taken in Biscayne Bay almost within the shadows of downtown Miami buildings.

Keeping a taut line on a fly rod catch is vital. Ted Lyman shows the correct technique.

3 / The Tackle

"ALTHOUGH THE BLUEFISH IS SUFFICIENTLY plucky to take a coarse troll, and few venture to angle for him with ordinary tackle, even with gimp snells, yet, with good bass-tackle and strong hooks, either wound with copper wire on a heavy gimp leader or snell, or with a hook fastened with wire to a piano string, capital sport is found still-baiting for them from a boat anchored along the edge of tide-ways in the estuaries and near the shores of bays."

So wrote Genio C. Scott in his classic, *Fishing in American Waters,* published in 1875. Scott would be amazed today to see the developments in modern marine angling tackle, but his basic observations concerning what is required for bluefishing still contain much that is applicable.

Consider first the strong hooks. This fundamental connection between the angler and his quarry is extremely important to fishing success, yet an incredible number of fishermen will scrimp and save a few pennies when buying a hook while they think nothing of spending many dollars just to reach the seashore. Investment in the best hooks available is a small one as far as cash flow is concerned, but is prime security when the battle with a bluefish is joined.

Any fishhook is a compromise of sorts. This compromise is between the hook's ability to penetrate and its ability to hold once it has penetrated. Basically, if the bite of the hook—that portion extending from the bottom of the bend to the point —is short, it will penetrate easily, but may not hold well. If the bite is long, the re-

verse is true. Over the years, the most popular styles used by bluefishermen have been the O'Shaughnessy, the Siwash, and the Eagle Claw type. The last named is primarily a hook for natural bait fishing.

As far as sizes are concerned, much depends upon the rod, reel, and line involved. For example, it would be impractical to terminate a fly fishing outfit with a 6/o hook, yet such a hook would cause no trouble when used with a stout boat rod. My own choices are for 4/o to 6/o hooks when fishing the high surf with a heavy outfit or when trolling for big blues; 2/o to 4/o hooks when casting with lighter gear or for light and medium trolling; 1 to 2/o hooks when waving a fly rod or light spinning rig around. It is perfectly possible to catch blues with hooks up to 8/o, but I can see no reason for such a monster. It is more difficult to set such a hook and, once set, it tends to button-hole. This means simply that the hook metal wears through the flesh of the fish to make a gap through which the barb may pass. When a bluefish jumps and shakes its head around, button-holing is a real cause for concern—at least for the fisherman.

When selecting hook sizes and styles, attention should be given also to the diameter of the wire from which the hook is made. In general, salt water hooks are graded in ascending wire sizes as follows: regular, strong, X strong, XX strong, and so on up to five X's. Since a large diameter wire will not penetrate as readily as a smaller one, it pays to keep wire sizes within reason. For all practical purposes,

X or XX of regular rounded wire are heavy enough for bluefishing. If forged—that is, with the bend hammered flat—an X strong hook will hold any blue I have hooked to date.

Material from which the hook is made is important. High quality tempered steel with a plating of tin over it leads the list at present in popularity. Such hooks hold their point sharpness well, stand up under pressure, and, eventually, rust. When a hook rusts, get rid of it. Cost of replacement is minimal.

Cheap hooks designed for salt water use are blued. They rust out quickly and I avoid them. Lacquered specimens are the so-called bronzed hooks, and those of black, used often for Atlantic salmon flies, are called Japanned. They will last in the ocean a little longer than the blued variety, but why use them when there are better alternatives? For the fly fisherman,

Frank Woolner with an inshore bluefish taken in Florida. He used a short braided wire leader.

there are now good stainless steel alloys available made by both O. Mustad and Son of Norway, and Wright and McGill Company of the United States. Because they do not rust, the fly dressing remains clean. It does not have to remain clean long, for the teeth of a bluefish will shred it to pieces long before the hook fails.

Although great progress has been made in the development of stainless steel hooks in recent years, those larger than 3/0 in size still tend to be brittle. This means that the point may break off right at the barb or the eye may split. Stainless models could be made today which would overcome these difficulties, but the cost of each hook would be too high for general sale. My guess is that this high individual cost will be brought down in the foreseeable future, and the tinned hook will thereby become less popular.

Various nickel alloys were tried for a time, among which were hooks marketed under the names of Z-Nickel and M-Nickel. Improvement in the quality of stainless has driven these off the general market because they will not hold a point and are basically soft. Other metals besides tin are used for plating—notably gold, silver, nickel, and cadmium. Gold-plated models are popular among natural bait anglers even though the gold wears off rather rapidly because of the thinness of the plated layer. Silver has never been popular in salt water, but the nickel and cadmium models, used widely on the Pacific Coast of this country, deserve wider acceptance among bluefish-

ermen. I personally opt for cadmium when a choice is offered.

Since the jaws of a bluefish are tough and armed with sharp teeth, hooks should be kept sharp at all times. Even new hooks should be touched up with a file or small carborundum stone. A file does the job more quickly. However, this sharpened steel rusts rapidly when exposed to salt water. By storing it in a watertight container—the plastic holder in which a toothbrush is sold is ideal—much of the rusting may be avoided.

Moving toward the angler in terminal tackle—I'm saving baits and lures for last —let me comment on leaders. Genio Scott's gimp snells, which were made from silk reinforced with wire, are a thing of the past. So is copper wire. Single strand stainless steel is the most popular bluefishing leader material today. Its strength is measured by gauge as indicated in the accompanying table.

Gauge Number	Diameter	Breaking Strain in Pounds
1	.010	20
2	.011	27
3	.012	32
4	.013	38
5	.014	44
6	.016	58
7	.018	69
8	.020	86
9	.022	104
10	.024	120
11	.026	140
12	.029	165

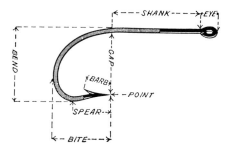

The various parts of a standard fishhook.

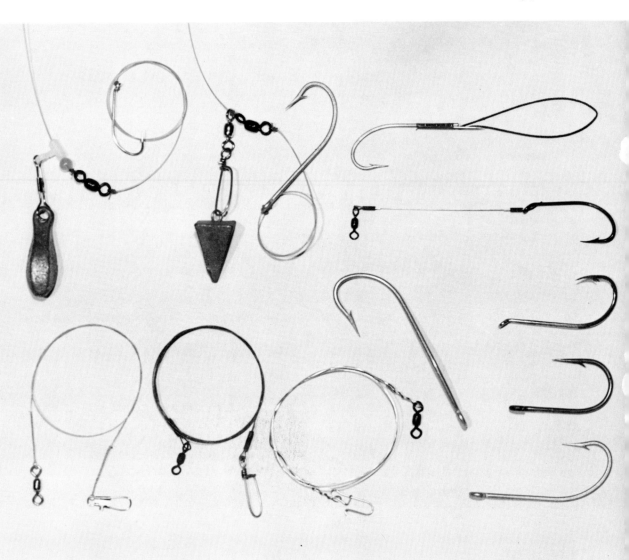

Bottom rigs, leaders, and hooks most often used in bluefishing. From left to right, top: bank sinker on fishfinder rig, best on rocky or rubbled ground; pyramid sinker with snap-swivel fishfinder arrangement. The pyramid weight holds well on sand, clay, or mud. Bait-saver hook and twisted wire leader: pin tied into hook-shank holds bait in place. Short, wire-leadered hook often used in a chum slick. Leaders, left to right, below: plastic-coated wire with locking snap; Seven-strand wire with bronze sleeves and Pompanette-type snap; stainless steel wire secured with haywire twist. Hooks are: bent long-shank, used in tube lures; then, top to bottom, far right, Claw, Siwash, and O'Shaughnessy.

From the practical fishing point of view, the actual breaking strain of higher gauge numbers is comparatively unimportant, for no angler, using balanced tackle, could put enough pressure on the largest blue that swims to part such a leader. What *is* important is whether or not a bluefish can bite through the wire. A hooked fish, if allowed any slack, often will chomp through the leader by doubling back toward the fisherman. In addition, its fellows may also take a swipe at the wire when trying to grab the lure or bait from the hooked fish's mouth. Finally, if the hook has been engulfed, the quarry keeps its jaws chattering madly and will cut itself free.

Some years ago, I beached a blue of about five pounds and ran some experiments on its wire-cutting abilities. Holding lengths of various leaders crosswise in its mouth, I found that gauges up to and including #4 would be severed cleanly. A bad crimp was put into #5, but it was not cut. I therefore suggest #6 as a minimum, and personally favor #9 to give extra insurance against the onslaught of real jumbos. Fortunately, no one was watching me during this experiment or they might have called for the men in white.

Obviously leaders should be matched with the over-all tackle being used. If using a light spinning outfit, #9 wire would be unnecessarily heavy and awkward to handle. A heavy leader also kills lure action to some degree. Water conditions also must be taken into account. Although blues rarely are leader shy, they may be when the ocean is clear and the sun is bright. As a general rule, it is wise to avoid stainless wire that has a bright finish. Stick with the dulled finish and not only will there be a chance of more strikes, but also neighboring bluefish will be less inclined to attack the leader.

Bluefishermen today are not limited to stainless steel single strand wire as leader material. Twisted cable now is manufactured with very small diameter and high tensile strength. This same cable coated with nylon provides a material of flexibility equal to regular cable and less tendency to kink. Even a length of very heavy monofilament may be used, although I prefer better insurance against the force of bluefish teeth. Finally, if the lure is comparatively long, as in the case of a large spoon or metal jig, it is possible to take blues with no leader at all, for the lure itself acts as a buffer against those snapping jaws. Examine the upper set of teeth on a big blue after it has been caught on a tinclad. Those needle-like choppers will be worn down to the gum line.

The length of the leader used also will vary with the tackle. A surf caster, using either a spinning or free-spool reel, will find that a leader longer than 20 inches presents difficulties on the cast itself. Casters using lighter outfits may have to cut this length in half. Trollers are virtually unlimited, but a leader longer than the rod tip length is unnecessary and makes boating of the catch difficult. Those who patronize party boats that toll in blues with chum often use a chunk of natural bait to attract the quarry. A special wire leader about three inches long, often snelled to the hook shank, is tied directly to monofilament line as protection.

Defining a leader exactly presents some problems. Casters using spinning gear often tie in a shock line, which is a length of heavy monofilament running from the leader itself down the entire rod length with a bit left over to make a couple of turns around the reel spool. It is a leader of sorts and prevents wear and tear on terminal gear.

There is also a light tackle wire line trolling technique in which the metal is tipped with approximately 100 feet of monofilament. To this mono is attached a normal leader. When fishing, all of the

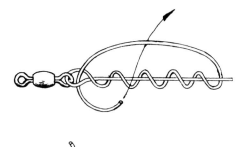

Improved clinch knot.

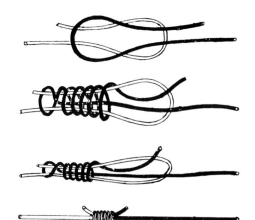

Key loop knot.

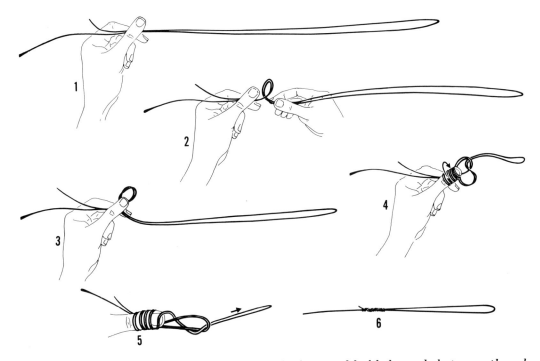

Spider hitch. (1) Make a long loop in the line and hold the ends between thumb and first finger, with the first joint of the thumb extending beyond the finger as shown. (2) Use your other hand to twist a smaller reverse loop in the double line. (3) Slide the fingers up the line to hold the loop securely, with most of the loop extending beyond the tip of the thumb. (4) Wind the double line from right to left around both the thumb and the loop, taking five turns. Then pass what remains of the large loop through the small one. (5) Pull the large loop to make five turns unwind off the thumb. Use a fast, steady pull—not a quick jerk. Pull the turns around the base of the loop up tightly and snip off the protruding ends of the line.

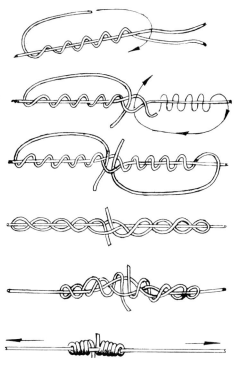

Blood knot.

impossible. Paul Kukonen of Worcester, Massachusetts, has made a science of taking blues on the long wand. He uses a tapered monofilament leader running from about 40-pound test at the butt to 15 at the tippet. To this tippet, he ties in a six to eight inch length of light stainless wire of #1 or #2 gauge. A regular haywire twist at both ends of this short wire is preferred to any swivel or snap mechanism. I have used the lightest obtainable nylon-covered cable as a tippet with success and, as Paul does, eschew swivels and snaps. A key loop secures this short leader-on-a-leader to the mono and a simple figure-of-eight knot holds the fly securely without kinking the metal-cored material.

My feelings about a clutter of snaps and swivels on any type of leader are strong. In my early bluefishing days, the standard leader sold by tackle shops had a heavy brass swivel at one end and an even heavier snap swivel at the other. The bright brass was an invitation to bluefish not hooked and they would often free their fellows by chomping on it. A small, dark swivel at the line end of a single strand wire leader makes tying-in of the line easy. A simple snap of the locking type at the terminal end facilitates changing lures. With nylon-covered cable, which I prefer over regular cable wire alone, line can be tied in with a key loop, thus dispensing with the swivel attractor. A crimped sleeve will do the same type of connecting job when regular cable wire is used.

Incidentally, when knots themselves are considered, I am not of the school that puts every knot used on the testing scale. The improved clinch works well for attaching line to a swivel or leader loop. If you want a double line for several feet above the leader, the Spider hitch is simple and strong. A simple figure-of-eight does the trick when securing nylon-covered cable to a swivel or snap. If my line is going to break, I want it to break close

mono is streamed, plus perhaps another 100 feet of wire—or whatever length is required to reach the proper depth. When a fish is hooked, the wire is recovered as rapidly as possible and the blue may then be played primarily on the softer line. A small swivel—small enough to pass through the rod's tiptop and guides—is used to connect the wire and mono. The true leader may then be joined either with another small swivel or with a key loop knot. Note that this leader will also be of lower pound test than that of the long shot of mono. It is simply insurance so that, if bottom is fouled, 100 feet of line will not stay down in Davey Jones' locker. This of course is a light tackle gimmick and does not apply to other types of fishing. It does serve to illustrate that leaders may well be a combination of items of varying lengths.

Fly fishermen have a special problem, for a heavy length of metal leader makes the presentation of a fly difficult, if not to the terminal tackle—namely, at the knot. Hopefully, this will never happen when playing a fish, but it may well happen when fast to an underwater snag. It is better to lose a bit of terminal tackle than half a hundred yards of line along with said terminal gear. The exception to this rule is when employing very light gear when every ounce of strength counts.

Lines themselves today may be divided into three major categories: the synthetic braids, which include most fly lines; monofilaments; and metal and weighted lines. Years ago, twisted linen Cuttyhunk was king for the sport fisherman, but it is rarely found now among modern anglers. The synthetics have taken over for several reasons. First, they are highly adaptable and may be manufactured with a considerable variation in characteristics. Second, raw materials from which they are made are plentiful and, unlike the old linen flax, quality can be standardized. In addition, they require minimum care and do not rot, although prolonged exposure to bright sunlight will decrease their strength. Finally, they can be sold at prices to fit almost any pocketbook. Let me emphasize, however, that it pays to buy products from nationally known manufacturers who will stand behind the lines they sell.

Shortly after World War II, braided nylon began to force linen out of the ocean angling picture as far as the caster was concerned. Made for use with a free-spool reel, the first nylon braids that were produced had too much stretch, poor knot strength, and, in many cases, were rough on the human thumb. By changing formulas of the basic filaments from which these lines were manufactured and by altering the tightness of the braiding, these difficulties were overcome to a large degree. Quality nylon braids today are still excellent for casting and also for trolling up to the 50 pound test class. Above 50 pounds, stretch presents a problem and, in addition, the line diameter is large for its strength.

The E.I. duPont de Nemours and Company, Incorporated—known to all and sundry today simply as duPont—then developed another polyester fiber which carries the name of Dacron. Also used on a free-spool reel, Dacron braid has less stretch than the equivalent in nylon, is a tough line, and has become highly popular for trolling. Although it may be used for casting also, I must admit that I find it hot under my thumb for such work.

Latest in the field is Micron, which is produced by the Cortland Line Company. With a very small diameter for its breaking strength, this line is basically coated Dacron and works well until the coating wears off. If an angler wants to pack a great deal of comparatively high test line on a trolling reel, Micron should be the choice. It is ideal for backing on a fly reel.

Monofilament braid is still turned out by some manufacturers for both free-spool and spinning reels. Today's product is far superior to the springy, stretchy mono braid of some years ago. It is abrasive under the thumb, but wears for an incredible length of time.

Monofilament itself was the reason for the boom in spinning after the end of World War II. Early European spinning reels were filled with fine braided silk line. The twists and tangles I threw into such lines in my youth could have best been cleared with a blowtorch. Today, monofilament not only has taken over the field in spinning, but also is well on its way to taking over in the free-spool area, up to and including big game fishing.

A tremendous amount of research has gone into the development of a wide range of monofilaments. Characteristics vary from very limp to very stiff, from colors of fluorescent orange to no color at all, from very cheap to comparatively expensive. You pay your money and you take your choice. A description of all the ad-

Choice of line depends on the fishing technique to be used. Shown here are synthetic Micron braid and depth-marked Monel; old-fashioned Cuttyhunk; round monofilament; oval mono; Dacron braid; forward-tapered fly line; single strand wire; and lead-core braid.

vantages and disadvantages of mono lines now on the market—and even some that may be on the market in the future—would fill a book in itself, so let me hit the high spots.

Those using spinning reels tend to over-emphasize the need for limpness in monofilament. It is certainly true that you do not want a stiff and springy line when spinning, or when using any other type of tackle for that matter. However, excessive limpness will result in line sloughs—loops of line pulling off the reel on the cast in a tangle. Selection is a matter of personal preference, but extremes should be avoided.

When filling a free-spool reel for either casting or trolling, mono that is slightly stiffer than that used for spinning is to be preferred. Be sure that the reel spool is designed for this type of line. Mono has "memory"—that is, when stretched, it

tends to revert to its original unstretched condition after strain has been relieved. This puts heavy pressure on a reel spool and may fracture it.

For conventional free-spool casting, I prefer mono that is oval rather than round in cross-section. My taste in this matter obviously is not that of the multitudes. Oval mono received wide publicity when it was introduced some years ago, many manufacturers turned it out, and sales were terrible! As a result, it is difficult to find in the marketplace today and, because I like it, my friends in the line companies classify me as an angling dodo. Oval, flat, or ribbon type monos are popular only among some light tackle plug casters and fly rod specialists, who use it as a shooting line. Do *not* use this line on spinning reels: it twists like a basket of eels.

As far as color is concerned, duPont has

Francis Davis fighting a bluefish with typical boat trolling tackle.

done a great deal of research in this area to come up with monofilaments in various fluorescent shades. These are more visible to fishermen, which helps in avoiding tangles when two or more fish are hooked simultaneously, and in following the movements of the quarry. Presumably they are less visible to the fish. This appears to be true in the case of fluorescent orange and yellow. However, bluefish must be unique when it comes to fluorescent blue, for they will attack the line itself. Perhaps they feel that the line is a form of spaghetti dinner—it's anyone's guess.

As is true with all other tackle items, it does not pay to buy cheap monofilament.

Careful examination of such material will show that the line diameter is uneven, which means it has weak spots. Buy the best and you will have no worries when a fish is hooked.

For the deep troller, single strand stainless steel or Monel alloy lines have gained acceptance all along the bluefishing front, even though the International Game Fish Association does not recognize catches made with such lines. For all practical purposes, 25-pound test wire is heavy enough for bluefishing. Charter skippers favor heavier metal simply because many of their clients may be amateurs who will break lighter stuff. Normally, a shot of 50 yards of wire at the most, backed with Dacron or other braid, will do the job.

Pick a metal-spooled reel when using wire line, for wire can ruin a plastic spool in short order. Also roller guides are recommended on the rod, since the wire will cut grooves in regular ring guides and tiptops. In brief, a special outfit should be set aside for this type of fishing.

A compromise of sorts when going deep may be made by use of lead-cored line. This is a nylon or Dacron braid woven over a center of flexible lead wire. It is bulky and does not cut down through the water as rapidly as single-strand wire, but it is easy to handle. In addition, a reel filled with lead-core may be substituted very quickly for another carrying regular braid or mono without fear of damage to the rod guides.

Fly lines of course fall into a special category of their own. A weight forward type, which used to be called a torpedo-head, is the choice. False casting and delicate presentation is not required when after bluefish. The aim is to get the lure out there in a hurry with the minimum of rod-waving. Floating lines, with or without a sinking tip, normally are used. However, a sinking line often will get better results, particularly in the fast waters of a tide rip. More difficult to handle than its floating counterpart, the sinker still is worth the trouble when trying to reach pay-off waters. A spare reel spool, entire reel, or complete outfit will make either choice available.

Fly line backing should be all the reel can hold. Micron or Dacron braids are best, and they should have a minimum breaking strain of 20 pounds. I personally prefer 25-pound backing as snag insurance. Never use monofilament for backing. Its memory factor, previously mentioned, will cause a fly reel to blow up like a bomb.

With line and terminal tackle in order, obviously the bluefisherman needs a reel and rod. The combination should be balanced, which does not mean that it tips like a scale when placed on a fulcrum a certain number of inches above the reel seat. Balanced tackle probably should be called matched tackle. Rod, reel, line, and lure form a combination that is practical for fishing, easy to handle, and effective for the job at hand.

Note that item—practical for fishing. I am not a stunt fisherman. I have no desire to hook a 30-pound bluefish on gossamer line with a toothpick rod and bore the poor creature to death over a four hour period. I enjoy light tackle angling as well as the next man, but neither I nor my fishing companions enjoy losing fish after fish in a vain attempt to land some world record on ridiculously inadequate tackle.

Before discussing balanced tackle as a whole, a few words on reels and rods in general should be recorded. Aside from fly casting, in bluefishing the free-spool and regular spinning reels are the two choices available. In the former, the reel spool rotates on its own axis; in the latter, the spool is stationary and line is laid onto the spool by means of a line pick-up device which rotates around the spool as the reel handle is turned. The closed-face spinning reel, often called a spin-casting reel, is not an efficient mechanism for salt water use, particularly when seeking large blues. It simply cannot cope with the effects of salt and the savage battle of a bluefish on a season-long basis. Certainly, it can be used—and is used by many on snappers and small specimens—but it does not meet the requirement of being practical for all fishing.

Free-spool reels fall basically into two classes: those used primarily for casting and those used primarily for trolling. Many models manufactured today can be used for both. Except in very light models, salt water reels today are equipped with a star drag, which is nothing more than a type of adjustable brake which allows pressure to be put on the fish while it is running out line. A lever, button, or other device permits the angler to disengage this brake on the cast, or while letting out line, so that the reel spool spins without restraint—hence the name free-spool. With the exception of some very light models, the salt water reel features an anti-reverse lock which prevents the reel's handle from spinning backwards. In early ocean angling, there was no such mechanism and the term "knuckle-duster," or even "knuckle-buster," was aptly applied.

Casting reels have a wider spool than those used for trolling. The reason is simple. When line is drawn rapidly off a narrow spool, the diameter of the bulk of line remaining on the spool is reduced very quickly. This results in fast acceleration of the spool itself—acceleration so fast that it is almost impossible to control. The wider spool gives slower and more uniform acceleration, which is more easily controlled on the cast without excessive braking action. Note particularly that line should be laid evenly on the spool while retrieving or advantages of width disappear. Level line devices are built into some models for this purpose, but I still prefer my left thumb for such work. To date, it has never become clogged with sand or gone out of order!

Spool materials on casting reels are normally lighter than those on the trolling models. Made of plastic, lightweight alloys, or a combination of the two, they present less inertia to overcome at the start of a cast than a trolling spool made from solid, heavy metal. They are also

Free-spool casting reels. (Top) Garcia Abu X Model 6500C bait-casting type mounted on a drop-center rod butt. (Center) The time-honored Penn Squidder surf-casting reel on a one-piece rod. (Bottom) The Penn Jigmaster, which has a fast retrieve.

slowed down and stopped at the end of a cast more readily. Some ruggedness is sacrificed, but the casting qualities are improved.

Another basic difference between casting and trolling reels is that of gear ratio between spool and handle. A caster often wants to have his lure moving rapidly the moment it hits the water, so models such as the Penn Jigmaster series and Garcia's Ambassadeur 5500C and 6500C have ratios of four-to-one or faster. For the troller, lure speed is controlled primarily by boat speed, so the ratio may be as low as two-to-one. Among reels normally used for bluefishing, it is slightly higher than this.

Unfortunately, reel manufacturers have never agreed on the standardization of numerals to indicate various sizes and line capacities of their products. A 4/o is larger than a 3/o in the same company's catalog, but there the accurate comparisons stop. Tabulation of the various types and quantities of line a reel will hold now is given in catalogs and literature describing the tackle, so reel capacity has evolved as the basic criterion of size.

If confusion among free-spool reels is bad, it becomes downright evil when the switch is made to spinning reels. Even within the same company, manufacturers' numbers apparently are allocated without rhyme or reason. Reel capacities are used to some degree, but the fact that many large spinning reels are used with a cork or plastic arbor on the spool to save winding on yards and yards of unused line makes such classification meaningless. In addition, one reel model holding

Trolling reels, left to right, include the 4/o Senator by Penn for heavy offshore work; the Penn Super-Peer with level wind; the Penn Master Mariner, chosen by many wire-line trollers. Roller guides, on the rod, should be selected when using wire.

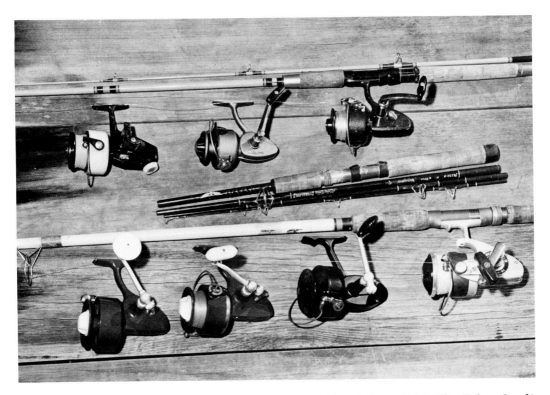

Spinning outfits range from light to heavy. (Top, left to right) The Zebco Cardinal, Browning, and South Bend reels with matching two-piece rod. (Center) A Fenwick four-piece rod for the jet plane traveler. (Bottom) Surf spinning reels include a manual-bail Penn Spinfisher, a standard full-bail equivalent, Mitchell 302, and a Daiwa mounted on a two-handed stick.

250 yards of 8-pound test mono may be far more ruggedly constructed than another holding exactly the same amount. Only by examining the reel itself can a fisherman tell whether or not it will suit his fancy and balance with the rod selected.

There are certain characteristics which should be taken into account when choosing a spinning reel for bluefishing. First, of course, it should be a model designed for ocean use. Fresh water models may well survive only a single trip in the ocean. The drag mechanism must be both smooth and tough. It is here that many spinning reels fall down. I personally do not care whether the drag control is on the face of the spool, at the rear of the reel housing, or elsewhere as long as it will operate properly and will not back off or

tighten up under its own power. In brief, once I set the drag, I want it to stay set until I choose to change it.

Positive bail action is also important. This means that the bail will close firmly to pick up the line when the reel handle is turned and will *not* close of its own accord on the cast. Some anglers have become so unhappy with automatic bails that they depend entirely on manual pick-up—a system whereby the line is picked up with the index finger and looped over a simple pick-up device that has no springs involved. I have no quarrel with these fishermen, for I have been caught far away from any tackle store with a broken bail spring. The bail itself hangs like a broken gull's wing and, if there is no replacement spring handy, fishing may come to a stop. However, I should point out that production models of manual pick-up reels today are few and far between. I therefore carry spare springs as a standard part of my equipment.

At this point in the discussion of spinning reels, I am going to make some enemies. Spinning was devised as a method of casting light lures. Spinning tackle is ideal for this type of fishing and I use it regularly. For trolling, however, the free-spool reel is far superior both in presenting the lure, in controlling it, and in battling the fish after it has been hooked. In high-surf fishing with heavy tackle, I also opt for the free-spool outfit. Once an angler has mastered the use of such gear, he will cast as far as, or farther than, one using a spinning outfit. More important, he will be able to handle a far wider range of lures weighing from two ounces up to as much as six.

Let me cite an example which will show when this ability may be important. Some years ago, I was surf fishing from the beach at Cape Hatteras, North Carolina. It was early in the season and the bluefish were deep, in fact they appeared to be feeding right on the bottom. My companion was a spinning enthusiast and claimed with considerable emphasis that a spinning outfit could outfish a conventional one any time, any place. I shield his anonymity because he still fumes when I remind him of that trip.

Try as we would, we could tempt no blue to hit an artificial lure. I then put on a five-ounce sinker, fish-finder rig, and a large chunk of cut mullet. Both wind and current were strong, hence the choice of such a large pyramid. I lobbed this whole, heavy terminal rig into the ocean and, within a matter of minutes, was fast to a bluefish of about eight pounds. Sure, I was over-gunned for the catch, but it and several that followed were at least catches.

My companion could handle a sinker

and bait combination also, but, even when he almost tore the top of his index finger off on the cast, he could just manage to toss a sinker-cum-bait combination weighing about four ounces, and this was tumbled down-current so rapidly he never had a strike.

Those who claim that spinning is the answer to any and all bluefishing problems often state flatly that they never use large lures or heavy sinkers and seem to imply that there is something vaguely unsporting about such rigs. Basically, of course, they are right—except for the unsporting aspect. They do not use such rigs for the simple reason that, with the equipment they have chosen, they cannot! Try casting a five-ounce metal jig or an eight-inch plug with a spinning outfit for half a day and you will see what I mean.

Switching to generalities on rods for the moment, no modern bluefisherman needs to be told that glass has taken over completely on the ocean front as a rod material. I still love the feel of a good split bamboo fly rod, yet glass is undeniably the modern king. The material requires minimum maintenance and it may be purchased in just about any length, diameter, action, and finish an angler might desire.

It is not within the scope of this volume to go into fine details on the manufacturing processes involved in producing a good glass rod. Suffice it to say that the best are of the hollow type, or hollow with a core of some other material. Solid glass is used widely for cheaper rods. Although perfectly satisfactory in shorter lengths, such as lengths used in the making of boat rods, solid glass does not have the versatility of hollow for good casting action. As I have noted before, you get what you pay for, so extra money invested at the outset means economy in the long run.

Ferrules, which are used to join one section of a rod to another, have long been the weak point in salt water rods and, in

addition, affect the action. When there is a choice, it is better to have the ferrule right at the leading end of the butt and the tip with no ferrule at all. The so-called weakfish or popping rods are so designed, and so are most modern boat rods. They should be the bluefisherman's choice.

To overcome this ferrule weakness and variation in action, Sevenstrand Tackle Manufacturing Company of California came up with a patented Feralite ferrule, which is used in the making of its line of Fenwick rods. One section of hollow glass is thrust into another, with the result that the ferrule is almost invisible, if such a joint can be called a ferrule at all. Other companies have followed this lead without infringing on patents. There is little question that, except for ferrules between a true rod butt and tip, the old, bulky metal ferrule dividing the tip into two or more sections will be phased out in higher quality rods during the next decade.

And so at last I come back to balanced tackle. The outfits I am about to describe are for practical fishing as previously noted. In many cases, the combinations may be considered heavy for bluefish. However, there is a reason for this. For example, a high-surf outfit has as its primary function the ability to cast a comparatively weighty lure from the beach to an area where blues feed. Once the quarry has been hooked, the tackle will handle it without difficulty. Undoubtedly, more sport would be had with a lighter

John Dunbar shows high surf spinning outfits. From left to right: 11½-foot tournament rod weighing 23 ounces; 11-footer of 25 ounces; a 10-foot, 8-inch rod weighing 27 ounces. The latter may look longer than the middle stick simply because it is closer to the camera.

outfit, yet the lighter outfit will not toss the hook into pay-off waters. A heavy trolling outfit will subdue even a world record bluefish without much strain. Often, however, a troller may be after other species and the bluefish catch will be incidental. He will not, for example, wish to lose a white marlin by using gear suitable for snapper blues. In casting categories, when I give lure weights, include natural bait and sinker combinations also. Writing "and/or bait and sinker" time after time—or reading it—becomes tedious.

The high-surf outfit is a specialty weapon designed to cast lures from two to six ounces for long distances in rugged water. It is at its optimum when using three- to five-ounce lures. For best results, the rod should be a one-piece job, which admittedly is difficult to transport. Overall length should not exceed 11 feet, and most average-sized fishermen will not be able to handle anything longer than 10½ feet. It is a common misconception among many surf casters that the longer the rod, the longer the cast. Such is not the case, and even a strong man rarely can get the full force of action from a 10½-foot glass blank. Mounted on the rod should be a good quality free-spool reel holding 200 to 250 yards of 30- to 45-pound test braid or monofilament. The heavier line is preferred when fishing at night when spooling is done by instinct rather than sight.

The standard surf outfit handles lures from about two to four ounces, measures

Conventional surf casting outfits are displayed by Claude Rogers. From left to right: 10½-foot Tidewater Anglers Club tournament rod, 36 ounces; Hatteras-type 10-footer, 24 ounces; 8½-foot jetty type, 21 ounces; 8-foot junior jetty, 20 ounces. All have stiff action and are primarily distance-casting rods.

9 to 10 feet overall, and mounts a free-spool reel holding 200 to 250 yards of 25- to 36-pound test braid or mono. Its equivalent in spinning may be six inches longer, with a reel capacity of at least 300 yards of 15- to 20-pound test monofilament. Heavier line can be used if desired, but will cut down distance on the cast.

The squidding outfit handles lures from slightly more than an ounce up to three ounces. Ideal for jetty fishing and boat casting when the going is rough, over-all rod length is about eight feet and the reel should hold a minimum of 150 yards of mono or braid. The spinning equivalent again may be six inches longer as far as the rod is concerned while the reel should hold about 300 yards of 10- or 12-pound test.

All the above are two-handed casting outfits and all have their place in bluefishing. However, in my opinion the closest thing to an all-purpose tackle combination for general casting under a wide variety of circumstances is a single-handed spinning rod approximately eight feet overall mounting a reel holding between 200 and 250 yards of 8- to 10-pound test mono. This rig will handle lures from the tiny midgets of a half-ounce up to a strong two ounces. It serves well for casting from both small and large craft, from shores of tidal rivers and estuaries—in fact from any area where blues may be found within a 50-yard radius in deep or shallow water.

The free-spool equivalent is a sea-going bait-casting rod—known in the old days as a weakfish model—with a tip not less than five feet in length and an extension butt which may be braced against the midriff during the battle. This extension butt, about 18 inches long, should mount a reel holding at least 150 yards of 15- to 20-pound braid or mono. Such a combination handles lures a trifle heavier than the spinning rig and is to be preferred if trolling as well as casting is involved. The popping rod, which is also excellent for bluefishing, is similar, but the rod tip may be as long as six feet. This combination is a favorite among pier and bridge anglers if the catch does not have to be derricked up from the water surface.

Lighter tackle combinations of course may be used, particularly when the angler is fairly certain that only small bluefish are available—a condition that cannot be anticipated regularly. If the target is bluefish, I rarely drop the line test below the eight-pound mark unless indulging in stunt fishing.

The last casting combination I will consider is the fly fishing outfit. If you want a lot of bluefish in a hurry, avoid it, but it can offer some excellent sport. Because there has been much publicity about catches of monster tarpon and similar semi-tropical species on the light wand, too many anglers feel that they must arm themselves with a man-killing, heavy weapon no matter what they plan to tackle in the ocean. Such is not the case. An 8- to 8½-foot rod with fairly stiff action calibrated to handle #7 or #8 line will do the trick. As noted when discussing lines, a weight-forward line is preferred, and fill the reel to capacity with backing of 20-pound test or more. Reel size should be large enough to take 150 yards of this.

In early salt water sport fishing days, trolling outfits were classified by the weight and length of the wooden rod tip, the length of the rod butt, and the thread count of the linen line used. With the advent of synthetics, this system went by the board and classifications are made on the breaking strain of the line in accordance with IGFA record categories. The heaviest of these normally used for bluefishing is the 50-pound outfit. Although it is heavier than required, many charter skippers have it as standard equipment because they know that some of their clients will break anything lighter—and a charter captain does not appreciate losing

Fly fishing tackle for bluefishing. The range is from heavy (top) to medium light.

expensive terminal gear because of ignorance or misuse.

The normal 6/o reel will hold between 400 and 500 yards of braided Dacron although, as I have mentioned before, capacities vary among manufacturers. For example, the regular Penn Senator in that size takes exactly 400 yards while the Garcia Mitchell #1060 can pack on 720 yards. Rod tip length is no less than five feet and the butt is approximately 18 inches. If wire line is to be used with this outfit or with any other trolling rods listed below, have roller guides and tiptop.

Better for bluefishing if 50-pound test line is required is a balanced combination with a 4/o reel, which can handle 250 yards or more. Dimensions for tip and butt as far as length is concerned are the same as for the heavier choice, but the tip

is of smaller diameter and has less stiff action.

More suited to bluefishing is the 30-pound rig with a 4/o reel as the heaviest. A smaller size is preferred, but it should have a capacity of about 300 yards of Dacron braid. Monofilament will also do the trick. Braid backing of about 50 yards is recommended to form a cushion against excessive strain on the spool. Again, the rod tip should be a few inches more than five feet with a butt of about 18 inches. Obviously the tip action will be lighter than with the 50-pound rod.

Standard big-game trolling rods such as those I have mentioned differ from what is called a boat rod in one major respect: the trolling rods all have a gimbal nock at the base of the butt, which fits into a fitting on a fighting chair or belt harness.

Boat rods, which are usual on the bluefishing scene, feature a rubber butt cap or similar device instead of the gimbal nock. In general, they are more lightly constructed throughout than the trolling rod.

Varieties are legion. They range from models with a seven-foot tip and two-foot butt to stubbies with tips of five feet and butts of 18 inches. Often manufacturers list particular models as "pier and boat rods"—and they are just that. If a flapping bluefish has to be hauled through the air for the last few yards of the battle, tackle must be strong. Similarly, a party boat angler should have an outfit heavy enough to keep considerable control over a hooked fish or he will make enemies on all sides.

Trolling combinations in the 20-pound and 12-pound IGFA classes are all based on a boat type rod and a free-spool reel, which should hold an absolute minimum of 150 yards of the line selected. I prefer at least 200 yards myself. Modern tackle catalogs feature balanced outfits in the manufacturers' listings and, since I am not paid by the word, I do not plan to list them all here. In general, the lighter the line, the lighter the tip in both basic weight and action. The many choices available are subject to the taste and skill of the individual angler.

Before leaving balanced tackle, let me mention one outfit that is neither balanced, standardized, lovely to look at, nor expensive. It is efficient. Youngsters over the years have used it with success to capture snapper bluefish, and as S. Kip Farrington, Jr., of East Hampton, New York, wrote in *Fishing the Atlantic* back in 1949, there is no better way of starting a youngster fishing than to take him or her snapper fishing. The outfit is simple—a long Chinese, Japanese, or even domestic bamboo pole, a length of line tied securely to its tip, and a baited hook. Even kids hardly able to toddle can handle such

gear with considerable success.

When I move on to the subject of baits and lures which will take bluefish, the horizon is limitless. Blues at times will eat just about anything. At other times, they will become highly selective to the point where they drive strong men to maniacal mutterings—or worse.

An example of this selectivity stands out clearly in my mind even though it happened many years ago. Joe Laffy, an outdoor writer of Lynn, Massachusetts, Kib Bramhall—artist, fisherman, and advertising director of *Salt Water Sportsman*—and I were surf fishing in the rips at Wasque Point on Martha's Vineyard. Blues were in those rips in numbers and were chomping bait at an incredible rate to the delight of screaming gulls and terns overhead. They completely ignored plugs, bucktails, and a wide variety of metal jigs.

Finally, I snapped on a Johnston jig, which looks much like a miniature sailboat hull with a hook swung from the point where the keel joins the hull itself. This jig, designed by Dr. Malcolm K. Johnston, at present of Temple, New Hampshire, unfortunately is no longer mass produced and my supply came from a handmade mold. With the first cast, I was fast to a bluefish. The process was repeated time and time again until I took pity on my companions and loaned them the only Johnston I had with me, which we all used in rotation. All of us took fish on that particular lure until the tide turned, and we did not even have a strike on any other offering.

Blues can be equally selective with respect to natural baits. A shrimp may do the trick one day and be worthless the next. Cut mullet might sweep the beach on Tuesday and be fit only for crabs on Wednesday. To discover just which bait works best at any point in time, a high-low rig, in which one hook is spaced about a foot from another, is a good device. Each hook can be baited with a different item until the proper combination is found. If limited to a single hook, present a bait cocktail—a chunk of herring tipped with a bit of seaworm, for example.

With whole baits, remember that a bluefish usually strikes at the head of any natural swimmer less than six inches in length, but will chop anything larger than that into pieces by striking at its mid-section. Hooks should be placed with this fact in mind.

When the fish are finicky, I make it a practice to cut open the first one caught to discover what its natural diet of the moment may be. Then, if possible, I try to "match the hatch" as fresh water trout anglers say. In any fishing with natural bait, make sure your own supply is as fresh as possible. Blues are not scavengers and like their meals firm and clean.

The history of bluefishing lures is a fascinating one. The so-called bone lure was a favorite back in the late 1800's and there was a sudden dearth of cats in Morehead City, North Carolina. A lucrative market was developed by boys who secured a dead cat—or a live one that was knocked on the head—buried the critter for a while, dug up the remains, and then sold the shank bones on the open market for 50 cents apiece. These bones are hollow. Cut into pieces about three inches long, they were slipped over a long-shanked hook and a wire leader was placed in the hook eye. The leader was then twisted around a broomstick to form coils. When drawn through the water minus the broomstick, the lure trailed bubbles and, due to the leader coils, had an erratic motion that was irresistible to bluefish. The future of the Morehead City felines was secured when it was discovered that turkey, goose, and chicken leg bones bleached in the sun worked equally well. Today, white plastic

Dick Hathaway beaches a bluefish at Martha's Vineyard that he caught with a Bob Pond Striper Swiper.

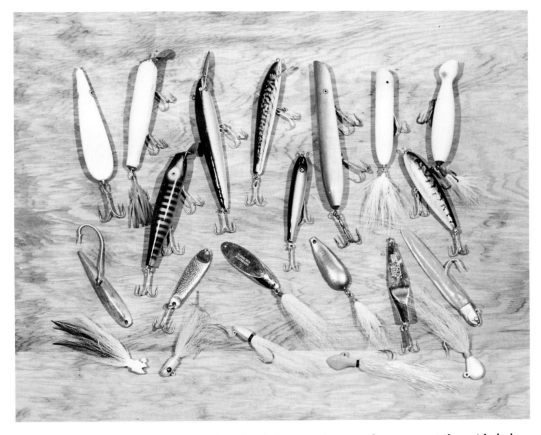

Typical casting lures used for bluefishing—plugs at the top, metal squids below them, and bucktails at the bottom.

and surgeon's rubber tubing have been substituted and the S.P.C.A. has no complaints.

Bluefish lures appear to go through cycles. Genio Scott had an illustration in *Fishing in American Waters* of a metal jig into which a piece of mother-of-pearl had been set. The lure disappeared for a time, then surfaced again in the 1940's with shimmering plastic in place of the mother-of-pearl. After the death of the manufacturer, who was a small operator as far as production was concerned, again it vanished from dealers' shelves. Then, in 1973, it once more reappeared with a design almost identical to that of Scott's sketch. Modern materials replaced the mother-of-pearl, but the lure still takes bluefish.

Heave-and-haul handline fishermen tossed metal drails made of lead and weighing a pound or more from the beach to take blues right up until the time when modern surf casting tackle was developed. This drail was undoubtedly the father of the metal jig or squid. Because lead tarnishes quickly in salt water, the lure had to be scrubbed with sand or scraped with a knife after a few casts to keep it bright. Some of these old heave-and-haulers, who coiled a hundred yards of stout marline pegged at one end in the sand at their feet, rubbed the lead with mercury, and the shine lasted. The next step was to make such lures of solid tin, and the name tinclad evolved. Now a wide variety of stainless steel and plated lures are available. Noteworthy among these are the Hopkins No-Eql lures of hammered stainless steel and the Acme Kastmaster, which is today's plated version of the old Eda Splune originally made from stainless.

Although tinclads are no longer made of tin because of the cost involved, any surf casting bluefisherman worthy of the name has a wide variety of shapes and sizes in his tackle box. Many designs have evolved over the years and often have been labeled in accordance with their point of origin as is the case with the Montauk Squid and the Point Jude Wobbler.

Cedar jigs with lead heads and wooden bodies were first used as bluefish trolling lures. A few are still available from those who craft them by hand, and they still catch fish. As tackle improved, it became obvious that these same cedar jigs could be cast. Salt water plugs, first developed by American Indians and then improved for taking weakfish in southern waters, might be considered to have cross-bred with the jigs. A whole new line of bluefish lures flooded the market.

Plugs are American in origin and Americans enjoy fishing with them. When a bluefish explodes under a surface popper, the reason is clear to see. Even though I have seen this happen countless times, I still am inclined to put tooth marks on my heart when the attack comes. Although the poppers get the most spectacular results, never neglect the subsurface models.

Because a plug is festooned with hooks, many believe that a bluefish will be taken more readily on it than on a jig with a single barb. Such is not the case. A bluefish can exert leverage against the plug body and tear itself free. In addition, one of its fellows is apt to take a cut at the lure visible in the hooked fish's jaws and part the line or leader.

Blues also are capable of grabbing a plug and avoiding all hooks. While fishing near Smith's Point off Nantucket with Bob Francis—bluefish and striper guide extraordinary—we were about to call it a day when a school of bluefish surfaced, chasing bait. We both tossed surface plugs to them; we both had strikes, which actually pulled several feet of line off the reel against the drag and drew the plugs underwater; then we both lost the fish. This happened not once, but several times. Eventually, we boated a couple by waving rod tips around violently after the strike. I still do not know how those blues dodged the steel barbs so consistently.

To give a wooden plug or metal lure the appearance of natural bait, fish skin was secured to the lure's exterior in the early days. It soon became evident that the common eel produced the best skin for this purpose and eelskin-covered jigs and plugs followed, along with the metal eelskin rig itself. This has a weighted, hollow head and water fills the skin tied around that head, so that the whole works swims in a natural manner. Bluefish will hit all such offerings as well as a whole rigged eel and plastic imitations, like the Alou. However, those bluefish teeth make short work of a soft lure. Repairs are annoying and frequent. Stick with the tougher models and you will save time and temper.

An excellent bluefish lure—and one often forgotten by modern anglers, perhaps because it originated in fresh water —is the spoon. I managed to keep this favorite secret weapon out of sight of rival bluefishermen for many seasons by tucking a couple of spoons into my pocket and leaving them out of the tackle box. Unfortunately for my reputation of bluefishing knowledge, others had long memories, too, and tried trolling spoons in the early 1970's. They worked. My secret weapon, which was really no secret at all, has become standard equipment for any serious bluefisherman. Good salt water spoons come in a wide variety of sizes, which is a great advantage when trying to match

Bluefishing flies and popping bugs.

the size to the bait upon which the fish are feeding.

Another general lure type should be mentioned, and again this is among the ancients of the marine fishing world. It is the feather or bucktail. The Japanese feather lure consists of a weighted metal head which has a hole in its center for a leader wire and hook. The head is decorated with feathers, plastic, crimped nylon, or some other material. The generic term of Japanese feather is now applied to many such trolling lures even though they may have no trace of Oriental origin and even less of feathers.

Similarly, the bucktail jig—also called leadhead—may be trimmed with all sorts of things other than bucktail. This is a casting lure primarily, yet it can be trolled or jigged in the depths. It features a weighted head so designed that the hook point rides upward and therefore does not foul on the bottom. Lures collectively called "bucktails" are among the most productive of all artificials, although, like the true Japanese feathers, they get thoroughly chewed and torn to bits by hungry bluefish.

Among modern lures which have become standard, I must include the Tony Acetta Jig-It-Eel and the Ragmop. De-

signed for trolling, their appearance will startle an inland trout fisherman to the point of numbness. The Jig-It-Eel is a lead-headed lure dressed with very long strands of crimped or straight nylon and comes in a variety of colors. The Ragmop features the same lead head to which is attached a light chain dressed with cross-tied lengths of soft, wriggly nylon fiber. Both lures are armed with two single hooks. For best results, these lures should be worked by jigging the rod tip while trolling.

A fairly recent development among commercial bluefishermen is the umbrella rig, which is actually a multiple lure. It was the outgrowth of the old Chesapeake Bay "Christmas Tree," which is a single spreader from which three or more individual lures are trolled on short leaders. The umbrella features two such spreaders rigged at right angles to each other around a central hook. They catch a lot of bluefish and, because the many hooks slash and tear the flesh of fish that are never boated, injure many more. So do nets. Strictly a meat fishing device, the umbrella is mentioned only because it is popular among some who want to fill the boat. Sporting it is not!

At the other end of the angling spec-

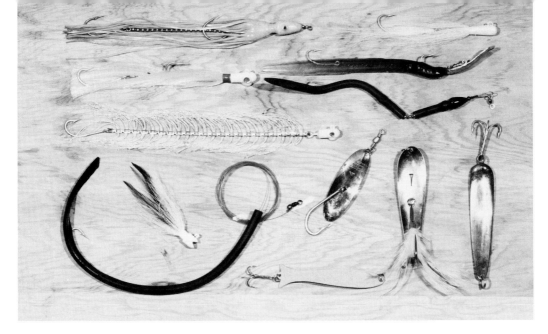

Trolling lures used for bluefishing.

trum is the fly fisherman, who specializes. Streamers and popping bugs are the favorites for blues, but there is no reason to present fancily dressed offerings. One bluefish catch will make mincemeat of it anyway! The trick is to match the size of the bait first and to try to match its basic color. Bucktail or similar material for the wing in plain white, or red, blue, yellow, green, or pink over white does as well as anything. Fairly bulky bodies of silver or yellow are preferred.

Long streamers tend to wrap around the hook bend on the cast. Paul Kukonen, who has been mentioned before, solves this problem by tying a short tuft of bucktail *under* the streamer wing, which holds the wing itself high and tangle-free. The resulting fly is unlovely, but it works. Popping bugs also work. However, choose plastic heads rather than cork, for blues will chew up the latter like popcorn.

Color in flies and in any other artificials can be important. When waters are murky or when light is dim, as at dawn and dusk, do not fail to try a lure that is basically yellow. In bright sunlight and in total darkness, on the other hand, yellow lures often are ineffective on bluefish. Red and white surface plugs will murder blues at times in areas below the Mason-Dixon line, yet I have had very little success with these in more northern waters. In general, blue, green, white, and silver are the basic colors, either separate or in combination, that appear to have the greatest appeal over a wide range. Black plugs used after dark can produce pleasantly surprising results. In brief, if one color combination does not result in a strike, try another.

Every season, some particular lure will take the lead over all others. Anglers happily decide that the solution to all their problems has been found. When the next season rolls around, the killer of the year before may be almost worthless and it is forgotten. My memory for such things is good and I always try out effective lures of the past from time to time. Sometimes, as in the case of the spoon, I hit the jackpot. More often, I catch nothing, but like the Count of Monte Cristo, I wait and hope. There is always another year coming.

Trolling for blues from a small charter boat.

4 / The Methods

A WELL-PLACED STICK OF DYNAMITE AND A well-placed fly made of feathers and tinsel will both take bluefish. Between these extremes, the choice of methods is almost limitless. As the old skipper who put clam juice in his drinking whiskey noted, it is largely a matter of taste.

In prehistoric times, old Uglug, the caveman, was fairly primitive in his approach to angling. Armed with a gorge, which is nothing more than a stick pointed at each end, and a length of twisted vine, he sank the gorge into a piece of bait, lowered it into the water, and then waited for fish to come to him. This basic approach still gets results, even with more modern tackle.

Often termed still-fishing, presentation of a natural bait to the quarry sought really is not "still" at all. Water moves around the offered meal as the currents flow; the angler may impart movement to the hook, and, at times, may cast bait and terminal tackle a considerable distance to reach the area where bluefish may be feeding.

The most simple method of bait fishing involves lowering a terminal rig—which includes sinker, hook, and bait—from a floating platform, such as a boat, or from some structure built over the water, such as a bridge or pier. Despite its simplicity, there are various refinements which should be noted to achieve maximum success. Remember always that a bluefish is a predator, not a scavenger. If the bait is not alive, it should be very recently dead or in a good state of preservation through quick freezing. Various pickling solutions, such as brine, may keep bait fish flesh in good enough condition for other species, but it does not work well for blues. Rigged eels and eelskins are the exceptions.

If there is a choice, I prefer a whole bait to one that has been cut into pieces. Bluefish tend to attack a whole fish, crab, or even seaworm, rather than a chunk of such offerings. Obviously, placement of the hook presents some problems. Let me repeat that blues normally hit the head of any bait less than six inches in length and the middle of longer foodstuffs. The hook should be located with this in mind. It is also possible to rig two hooks in tandem to cover a wider strike area.

Any bait should be rigged to make it look as natural as possible. Even a cut chunk of mackerel may be given some additional appeal by moving it along the bottom or off the bottom with rod tip action. A small float between the hook and sinker often helps, for it will move the bait around slightly with the current. Some anglers color such floats so that they act as attractors in themselves. Tackle manufacturers are aware of this and several colored floats, such as the Fireball, are available on the commercial market.

Arguments among bait fishermen rage around whether or not the sinker should be rigged above the hook so that leader and bait trail from it to move naturally in the current, or below it so that the slightest nibble may be felt, unhampered by the sinker weight. Frankly, when still-fishing for blues, I have never found that there is a great deal of difference as far as results are concerned. I normally shoot for the best of all possible worlds by having one hook rigged above the sinker and another below it.

Live bait falls into a special category. Obviously the main purpose of using an active crab, herring, or other sea creature is to make the offering appear as natural as possible—and alive! The hook, therefore, should not be driven through some vital part of the bait's anatomy. Sinkers or other weights must be kept to a minimum. If it is necessary to go deep, place the weight between line and leader rather than close to the live bait itself—or use wire. The bait will then be able to swim with as little restraint as possible.

If a live bait dies, do not despair. It is still fresh and has plenty of bluefish appeal. This was illustrated clearly some years ago when Larry Nickerson, Charlie Letson of Madison, Connecticut, and I were fishing off a jetty in Larry's home waters at Harwich Port on Cape Cod. I was unable to hook a bluefish of any kind, but the others had strikes, or beached fish, using live alewives, which Larry had taken from a nearby stream which they were ascending to spawn. Alewives have little stamina and our supply of active bait soon became completely inactive. Using the dead article, however, produced continued results for all concerned, including my own special results of no fish at all. You can't win them all!

Surf fishing with bait, either alive or dead, can be compared in general to still-fishing, with the obvious difference that the angler must toss terminal gear seaward in order to reach the quarry. Because of this, any bait must be secured firmly on the hook or it will spin away into the ocean with no connection to the caster. With soft-bodied critters, such as clams, light thread or a fine rubber band helps prevent this accident. Impale the bait with the hook point, then secure it to the shank and eye with the wrapping.

I personally favor a fish-finder rig for all presentations of natural baits while surf fishing, and, in many cases, while fishing from a pier or boat also, when blues are feeding close to bottom. This device is really a sophisticated sliding sinker attached between line and leader. If you are fresh out of fish-finders, a snap swivel will serve the purpose. The line is slipped through the swivel ring and the sinker is attached to the snap. A swivel on the end of the leader snubs up against the fish-finder on the cast, but once the sinker rests on the bottom, a fish may pick up the bait without feeling the sinker's weight. If line is held without slack, the slightest nibble will be telegraphed up it to the rod tip.

Besides still-fishing, another more or less passive method of presenting a natural bait to bluefish is drifting. From a boat, the angler allows his craft to move with the current and a baited hook moves along with it. This system is not recommended in areas where the currents are strong—often areas where the bluefish are plentiful! It also can make instant enemies if many boats are fishing by other methods in any given chunk of ocean. A drifting craft is basically out of control and thereby becomes a navigational hazard, particularly if the skipper is fast to a fighting bluefish.

In gentle currents, when there is plenty of sea room, drifting can be amazingly successful in locating blues. In the early season, when the fish normally are deep, any type of natural bait may be bumped along just off the bottom. When there is a strike, have the anchor ready to be eased over the side without making a tremendous splash. If a sinker is used, again have it rigged between line and leader so that the bait rides naturally. I choose lead-core or a short shot of wire line over any type of sinker for this type of fishing.

Night party boat fishing off the New Jersey coast. Chumming with menhaden brings the blues close to the boat, and often eight or ten fish are hooked simultaneously.

Keep "feeling" for bottom—that is, let out line at regular intervals until you are sure that the hook is near the ocean floor, then reel in a foot or two. Some terminal gear may be lost, due to snagging, and the system therefore is not recommended over very rough and broken bottom.

When drifting, a whole bait or a strip cut from a fish—even from the belly of a bluefish—is better than a cross-section chunk. The fluttering action has particular appeal when drifted slowly. Pork rind may be substituted if natural bait is not available.

True artificials are also effective. The term "spin-jigging" was coined in Florida

79

Butterfish make a good bait for fishing in a chum slick. Cutting one fish as shown produces two baits.

for a particular refinement of drift fishing. As the boat moves down current, a cast is made with a bucktail type lure from the *up-current* side of the craft. The lure is then allowed to sink with a free line until it hits bottom. The retrieve is slow and the rod tip is lifted smartly after every two or three turns of the reel handle. This causes the lure to hop along the bottom. Blues at times will follow a jig presented in this manner right to the surface and will snatch it just a moment before it is lifted from the water. It therefore pays to fish out every cast right to the end.

I use a modification of this system even when trolling. Frankly, I become bored with trolling after a time when action is slow. Then I may be found on the foredeck of the trolling vessel casting ahead and slightly to one side of the bow with a deep running lure. As the boat steams up on the sinking hook, I reel just to keep a tight line. Then, when the line is roughly abeam, I start jigging and reeling. Many times I have picked up bluefish which apparently have ignored the trolled offerings.

Drift fishing is not confined to the bottom zone by any means. If several anglers are aboard and blues have not been located, have each fisherman try a different depth during the drift. Once pay-off waters have been discovered, all can then shift to them. If trying one particular

area, such as a known shoal, do not steam back up-current right through the good water. Give it a wide berth and then kill the engine when in the proper position to start again.

Shore-based anglers cannot drift, but they can make use of a current to do the job for them. From the bank of a tidal river or estuary, from a bridge or pier, a bait—with or without weight—is dropped into the water and allowed to move with that water while line is let out. When the desired section has been covered, the offering is then reeled back slowly with action given to it by twitching the rod tip. When no sinker is used, this method of fishing is called live-lining. No one has yet come up with a similar term if a sinker is added, but "lead-lining" might be appropriate. Note that, as the bait is being drifted down current, the line should always be kept taut. Blues may hit at any time—and a great loop of line swinging loosely will result in a missed strike. As is true when drift fishing from a boat, artificial lures as well as live and dead natural baits may be employed.

A particular form of live-lining yields literally tons of rod-and-reel bluefish each season off the northern New Jersey coast. Craft ranging from unsafe outboard skiffs of too small a size for ocean work to large party boats with all modern safety equipment aboard stud the sea by day and night during the peak season.

Grinding menhaden for chum is standard practice aboard the party boat bluefishing fleet.

They anchor, and crewmen ladle chum over the side. The usual chum is ground menhaden—known to the locals in that area as mossbunker, or simply bunker—and fish gather to obtain a free meal. The quantities of this chum are so great that many gourmets claim, with some truth, that bluefish toward the end of the season acquire a definite taste of menhaden oil when prepared for the table.

A good chum slick is obtained by ladling small amounts of ground fish or other enticer over the side at frequent intervals, not by dumping gobs of the stuff into the ocean every five minutes. Bait can be a piece of the chum itself. If finely ground, a half handful can be dropped into a piece of nylon stocking or milady's hairnet and then tied to the hook with fine thread. Be sure milady does not want to use either the stocking or the hairnet ever again! For reasons best known to the bluefish, a bait of some totally different kind often will give better results—as will artificials. Although I have maintained previously that a whole bait is usually better than a cut one, many anglers do very well with chunks of butterfish or menhaden when chumming.

Unless fishing from your own craft or with understanding friends, do not use light tackle when chumming. One hooked blue that races around and about in the slick will spook others, and will also tangle every line within swimming range. Another way to court sudden death at sea is to run at high speed through another boat's chum line, or to anchor just down current. Any angling judge will find for the defense under such circumstances. It is an obvious case of justifiable homicide.

Why chumming for blues has not spread farther on the angling coast has long been a mystery to me. Milt Rosko, writer and angler of New Jersey, tells me that night chumming with pieces of shrimp at the oil rigs and sulfur wells off Grand Isles, Louisiana, is now popular. A few surf and small-boat fishermen lay what might be considered private chum slicks by filling a bag or screened box with ground fish and hanging it from a rope in the vicinity of their hooks. Obviously the surf man must have fairly calm water and an offshore current to make this system effective. However, in general, chumming is not a widely used method. When those involved cooperate, it will bring bluefish close aboard to feed either on the chum itself or on bait which is attracted to the free handout.

Statistics are not available on the point,

but my guess is that trolling is the most popular method for catching bluefish along all coasts. A newcomer to the ocean front is able to take his share of fish if he keeps the rod tip up and has strength to reel. Basically, there are three primary factors to be considered when trolling: speed of the boat, depth of the lure or bait, and the lure or bait itself. They are all closely interrelated. An additional factor, which seems to bother neophytes more than it should, is the amount of line streamed from the reel. As I hope to explain in a moment, this varies. In brief, there should be enough line out to reach the fish.

Blues have been known to hit lures trolled at speeds in excess of 20 knots, but I do not recommend burning fuel at such a rate. On the average, speeds ranging between five and eight knots may be considered to be ideal under normal conditions. When fishing deep—that is, when the hook travels 50 feet or so below the surface—select a rate at the lower end of this range. Fast travel, when a heavily weighted terminal rig is being used, puts a tremendous strain upon line, rod, and even the angler. In addition, when the boat is slowed or stopped for the ensuing battle after a strike, chances are good that there will be slack line. Bluefish take full advantage of such slack and shake the hook.

Speed should also be varied to allow for current. For example, if trolling with a five-knot current at a speed of five knots, the lure tends to sink and to move through the water with very little action. Conversely, when trolling against the same current at the same speed, both the boat and the lure will be stationary with respect to the bottom while water will move around the lure at five knots. It is as though the boat were anchored, yet it may be maneuvered so that the hook covers a considerable amount of water as the craft is angled across the current. If there

Bob Hutchinson with a 16-pound bluefish caught while trolling off Cape Henry.

Trolling has produced this bluefish which is being brought to gaff.

is a choice—and there usually is—troll against the current or across it at a slight angle, rather than with it.

Angling across a current in this manner can be developed into a fine art when fishing tide rips. Blues tend to hang in the area a few yards down-current from the visible surface of the rip itself. The boat should be a minimum of ten yards from this sighted rip and the angler should let out enough line so that his lure passes through the pay-off water. Experienced skippers can troll a rip in this manner within spitting distance of one another without collisions or line interference. When the end of the rip is reached, the boat concerned speeds up, heads up-current, then proceeds to its original starting point to repeat its run. One of the quickest ways known to make bluefishing enemies is to turn down-current and steam through the edge of the rip, thus spooking every fish in the area.

Obviously, current force will be directly related to the speed of trolling. When there is little or no current, the five- to eight-knot rate is recommended, and do not be afraid to vary the speed when there are few strikes. There are exceptions to the recommended rate. Although mullet are not known for their swiftness, blues feeding on them seem to prefer a fast-moving lure. Move the throttle up a notch or two when the mullet are in and results will improve.

During the early season, or at other times when blues are feeding at or near the bottom, slow down so that the hook travels only a foot or less over the ocean floor. Sinkers, wire, or lead-core line will take the lure down. In the Race, a well

E.R. "Spider" Andresen rigs a line to a deep trolling device used when the angler wishes to have no sinker weight on his line. When a fish strikes, a trip mechanism releases the fishing line from the weighted one.

known bluefishing area off the eastern Connecticut shore, anglers often combine wire line with a shiny sinker to get deep in a hurry. The sinker itself attracts fish to the lure, which trails astern on a two- to four-foot leader.

Rarely is it necessary to stream dozens of yards of line when fishing at or near the surface. Blues generally are not line or leader shy, and they often zero in on the wake of a boat to see what the commotion is all about. In shallow water, however, the wake may have an opposite effect and will spook fish for yards around. Therefore, troll with a long line and at slow speeds on the shoals.

If the fish are breaking, *never* troll directly through the surfaced school. It is possible to pick up a chopper or two when this is done, but a majority of the blues will scatter. The loom and shadow of the boat, with a possible assist from propeller wash right over their heads, will put them down. Maneuver the craft so that lures pass along the edge of the school rather than through it. School chasers, who steam at full throttle toward any surfaced fish, can ruin chances not only for themselves, but also for any anglers in the vicinity. When blues are popping up and down, chances are good that they will be back in the general area where they first surfaced. Keep trolling, if possible in the direction towards which the fish were heading when last sighted.

In open water when landmarks are out of sight, it is often difficult to pinpoint the spot where a school has been. A handful of chum, which gives out a visible slick, a piece of crumpled paper, and even a teaspoonful of common, powdered dye will serve to help relocate the area. In these days of pollution awareness, I recommend against using plastic markers for this purpose unless they are taken back aboard later. What the U.S. Navy calls a retiring search plan then follows. Simply head due north from the marker for 50 yards. Then turn east for another 50, thence south for 100, west for 150, north again for 200, and finally east again until you get discouraged. You may also circle the area in ever-increasing spirals, but the course changes at right angles are more easily controlled by the helmsman.

Since blues often do not cooperate by showing themselves, the troller must take his chances in known good areas, such as tide rips or along the beach surf line. This last, incidentally, does not mean the point where waves are breaking, but where waves make up before they break. When close to shore, ranges may be taken on landmarks to relocate pay-off areas.

Modern electronic equipment has been a great boon to the offshore bluefisherman. Loran and radio direction finders make it possible to pinpoint prime feeding grounds. When marked on a navigational chart, such spots may then be revisited hours—or even weeks—later. In such recording, note the stage of tide and direction of current when success was greatest, for blues will shift their position with current changes.

The depth-sounder has become an almost indispensable piece of equipment for those who concentrate on boat fishing. With it, an angler can locate reefs and seamounts which, three decades ago, could only be found by careful piloting and manual soundings. Flickering dials and recording paper give a picture of the sea floor as a boat runs on any given course. This makes it possible to present a lure on the down-current side of some unseen underwater slope where the choppers lie in wait for tumbling bait fish.

Furthermore, on sophisticated dials or traces, you can spot the fish themselves and figure their precise depth. Those familiar with their equipment can even give an excellent estimate of the size of the blues swimming under the boat's keel. With experience, the tiny blips of light or marks on the recording roll can be translated into fish in the box.

Depth-sounders, which have been modified so that the sonar beam may be trained at all sorts of angles other than the perpendicular, now are available within a reasonable price range. These have the advantage of making it possible to scan a wide area underwater all around a fishing craft. Choice between portable and permanently installed equipment is dependent mainly on the size of the boat, with skiff and small-craft owners opting for the portable gear in general. No matter what the choice, there is no question that a good depth-sounder is a basic weapon for the boatman.

Some bluefish trollers have gone back in history and do their fishing from sailboats, thus combining two sports in one. I have tried this method with Dr. John Homans of Brookline, Massachusetts, while fishing off the Block Island coast in Rhode Island. There is no question in my mind that a surfaced school of blues can be approached more closely in a sailboat than in a powerboat, and the school does not seem to be disturbed by the boat itself. When several hook-ups occur simultaneously in a brisk breeze, things can become a little frantic!

Before leaving the subject of trolling, let me say that my scant hair curls when I hear a bluefisherman say that he set the hook "again and again" after a strike. This is one of the best ways known to man to break up tackle and tear hooks from the fish's mouth. When you are trolling at high speeds, blues will set the hook themselves, and will do so nine times out of ten even at low speeds. This can best be illustrated by the fact that thousands of bluefish are hooked each year on unattended rods left in a rod holder. It is an instinctive reaction for any angler to lay back on the rod when a hit is felt, and no damage is done. Repeating the process serves no useful purpose and may well end in disaster.

In the ranks of bluefishermen, the surf caster holds a place apart. Often bewhiskered and sleepless, always a little contemptuous of those who depend upon "stinkpots" to reach their quarry, he feels that he combines the virtues of both hunter and fisherman. There is some truth in this attitude, for a surfman must have good knowledge of beaches, tides, currents, habits of bait, and bluefish themselves, or his quest will be unsuccessful. Confined to a limited area, when compared to the boatman, he must make the most of all opportunities.

Note, in my definition, that there is a difference between a surf fisherman and a surf *caster*. The former is one who fishes from the beach by any means, with natural bait or with artificial lures. The latter is more specialized: he casts and retrieves artificial lures only. Years ago in New Jersey, metal lures were termed "squids," even though they had little resemblance to the natural bait. "Squidder" and "squidding" have survived in the angling lexicon, despite the fact that plugs are used widely today. A squidder, therefore, is a surf caster—and *vice versa*. Purists may claim that a true squidder uses a free-spool reel, not a spinning reel, but I eschew this distinction.

Being able to read the water, so that good spots may be distinguished from bad, and being able to cast accurately to a desired point, are the two prime requisites for a good surf caster. The ability to cast a long line comes in a poor third. Distance casting is a nice skill to have, of course. When blues are at extreme range, it means they can be reached. More important, when long distance casts have

When you are looking for bluefish, get high. Although a rooftop normally is not handy, in this case it is being used to spot working birds over the fish. Waders are not absolutely necessary!

Nantucket surf fishermen.

been mastered, shorter ones can be made with less effort and with more accuracy. Those who specialize in trying to reach Spain with their lure all too often fail to fish that lure carefully right back to the beach edge. If they have a strike after half the line has been retrieved, they will claim that the bluefish followed the lure inshore. In point of fact, they may well be fishing beyond the point where the blues are lying and would improve their luck if they shortened their casts.

As is true when trolling, speed, depth, and the lure itself are basic to success. Newcomers to surf casting worry a great deal, even as I did years ago, about the exact speed at which a lure should be retrieved. As a starting point with a free-spool reel, turn the reel handle about once a second when fishing with a metal jig. The rate should be lowered slightly when spinning since the ratio of handle to bail with such tackle is higher. Since it is almost impossible to check a stopwatch while surf casting, count out loud: "one, chimpanzee, two, chimpanzee" and so on. The interval will be about one second. Neighboring anglers may think you are a refugee from an animal farm, but ignore them.

When plug fishing, retrieve at a rate that will keep the line tight at all times. This is not difficult when using underwater and sub-surface lures. With surface poppers, it can present problems. The lure should be twitched with the rod tip to make it pop and, instantly afterwards, reeling should be speeded up to take in slack line. Some anglers—I am not among them—waggle their rods violently like a boy shaking a small apple tree throughout the retrieve to impart action to a pop-

Beach buggy fishermen waiting for the tide to turn.

ping plug. This method works without question, but I find it exhausting and, when there is a strike, confusing and uncontrolled.

Normally when bluefishing, the lure should be moving toward the beach the moment it hits the water. This can be accomplished by lifting the rod tip the moment the reel's gears are engaged. If you are not waist-deep in water or teetering on the edge of a rock jetty, a step backwards will help. There are exceptions to this general rule. If the blues are deep, it may be necessary to let a tinclad sink down to their level even before the gears are engaged on the reel. When the current is swift and when the lure is the bucktail type, fish may be caught by engaging the gears, then not retrieving at all. Let the lure swing with the current on a taut line until it reaches slack water.

This same system may be used to some degree with plugs. However, with surface models, twitching the rod tip will give the lure more appeal. Also, when plug fishing, the exact target, such as a knuckle in a tide rip, may have been missed. The lure may then be allowed to float a yard or two until it reaches the desired spot, at which time the retrieve is started normally.

Knuckles in tide rips—points where the currents clash in such a way that a small whirlpool or back eddy is formed—are prime bluefish producers. At times, it seems as though every blue in the county is lying in an area only a couple of square feet in size. Once on Monomoy Point on the southern spur of Cape Cod, Frank Woolner, Bim Simmonds, Ted Lyman, and I were casting for blues in the late afternoon. Frank had been making dis-

paraging remarks about the fighting ability of bluefish and their readiness to hit any and all offerings. We had covered the rip fairly thoroughly with no results when I dropped a jig into one particular knuckle. Immediately I was fast.

As I fought the fish and moved downcurrent, Ted stepped into the exact spot from which I was casting, dropped a lure into the same knuckle, and also was fast. Bim followed suit, by which time I had beached my catch. I moved back into line before Frank realized what was going on. After three of us had beached or lost a couple of fish apiece, we took pity on him and let him into the winner's circle. He cast to the knuckle, a fish was on, and the point was made that blues can be very particular indeed as to just where and when they will take a lure.

This also demonstrated that surf casters, working together, can fish a small area without interfering with one another. By timing casts carefully so that two lures are not in the air at the same time, or falling across a line that is already in the water, a number of anglers may fish practically shoulder to shoulder. Let one of them get out of cadence and the results are unhappy. The person who jams his way between two other fishermen on the beach and casts like a windmill will soon find himself without friends.

When a bluefish is seen to miss a lure or hit without hooking, there are two major avenues open to the surf caster, and to any other type of fisherman for that matter. The first is to drop the rod tip, give a little slack line, then start to retrieve. The second is to jerk the lure forward, then reel like mad and give it all the action possible. In actual practice, I usually combine the two options. I drop the rod tip momen-

Fishing the Nantucket surf as boats offshore troll the rips.

tarily so that, if the fish has turned, it will have a chance to hit again where it first missed. Then I lift the tip smartly and reel rapidly.

When trolling, a lure will pass over a bluefish once only, until the boat is turned and the lure is presented again after a considerable interval. When surf casting, a lure may be presented to the same fish several times within a few minutes. This has its advantages. The late George Bonbright, who made a name for himself in light tackle fishing during the early 1900's in Florida, used to travel by dory to the tide rip off Great Point, Nantucket, armed with a split bamboo two-handed salmon rod and large streamer flies. Since outboard motors had not been invented, his means of propulsion was two stalwart oarsmen, who must have disliked bluefishing forever after.

Bonbright would stand in the dory while the rowers held the boat in position against the current. He could see bluefish through the clear water lying, as he said, "like lead pencils" in the rip. He reported that often on his first cast to a particular fish, there would be no evidence that the blue had even seen the fly. On the second cast, the fish might stir. On the third, Bonbright would brace his feet, for a hit almost always followed. In brief, a lure presented to a bluefish time and time again may well aggravate it into attack. For this reason, when I am working along a beach, I always make at least three casts from the same position before moving on a few yards.

When there are no other anglers in the neighborhood, remember to cast at various angles, not just straight out to sea. Often a blue will take a swipe at a lure moving nearly parallel to the breaker line when it will ignore one traveling a perpendicular path. This is particularly true if there is a strong current running along the shore.

The surf caster utilizes tackle that is

Be and Win Allen fish the Wasque Point surf without getting in each other's way.

heavier than needed to beach a bluefish simply because it must be heavy enough to toss the lure into good water. As when trolling, the rule of *keep the fish coming* applies. If a blue jumps after being hooked, ignore the advice given by those using light tackle on tarpon: do not bow to the fish and dip the rod tip. Keep the line tight and chances of beaching the catch are improved. And be prepared for a jump right in the wash when the bluefish feels sand under its belly.

When fish are breaking within casting range, drop the lure just ahead of the school, if its direction of movement can be determined. In other cases, aim for the inshore edge. It is perfectly possible to hook a bluefish by casting beyond, or into the middle of, the flurry, but chances of taking another thereafter are reduced. The hooked battler will rush about among its companions and the line is apt to strike them, and thus alarm them, so that the whole school takes off for parts unknown.

Let me emphasize that there are no fixed rules concerning speed of retrieve, depth of lure, or type of lure itself. Be flexible. If one speed, depth, or lure does not work, try another. Imagination and experimentation are just as important to a good surf caster as they are to a good research scientist.

Casting from shore is not limited to the high surf by any means. There are times when bluefish in a feeding frenzy come right into the wash and even strand themselves. In 1971, along the Outer Banks of North Carolina, beach walkers gathered in an amazing number of blues without benefit of hook, line, rod, or reel. In their gluttony, the fish would beach themselves pursuing frantic bait on an incoming wave. As the wave receded, all that was required to collect an evening meal for the people on hand was a gentle kick that sent a bluefish flopping above high tide mark. At times, even a fly rod may be used in the surf, but don't count on it.

Blues are attracted inshore by bait. If the bait is beyond casting range, the angler must go out to meet it. Such a system has been developed to a fine art along the New Jersey coast. I do not mean by this that Jersey bluefishermen have aquired such divine qualities that they can walk on water: they simply clamber out on the many jetties which are found along that part of the coast. Marine growth covers such jetties, currents and eddies suck around them, bait fish gather, and the blues follow.

Jetty jockeys basically have become highly specialized surf casters. This method of fishing is not a game for the old and feeble, nor for those who have a poor sense of balance. Tackle is lighter than that used in the high surf, yet even such tackle is hard to handle when perched atop a slimy chunk of granite which may be ankle deep in water at one moment and waist deep the next. Metal hobnails or creepers on wader soles are part of the uniform of the day—or night. The trick is to get out on the jetty at the proper tide and, even more important, to get back before the tide rises to cut you off from dry land.

In general, the basics which apply to all surf casting apply also to jetty fishing. However, long casts as a rule are not needed. At night especially, bluefish may appear literally at your feet. On one occasion in the Point Pleasant area of New Jersey, I learned this the hard way. I had just decided that a chunk of rock a few yards along the jetty looked more enticing than the one I was standing on. Doing a balancing act, I extended my jetty rod parallel to the water to serve in much the same way as a tightrope walker's pole does. Incidentally, this is a good trick under normal circumstances, even when wading, for the rod slapped down on the water surface can restore balance.

Foolishly, I had not secured well the plug I was using. It dropped into the suds close to the jetty, and a bluefish that disliked me grabbed it. The yank of the strike tumbled me head over heels in the middle of a stride. I saved the tackle. I saved myself. I did not save the bluefish. For some time afterwards, my thoughts were on my bruises and were far away from bluefishing!

That lesson has never been forgotten, even though the scars have healed. If it happened to me today, I might well not be writing this book, since my bones are more brittle than they were in my youth. I do not bounce off granite as well as I did. At any rate, when I cast from a jetty, I fish that cast right up to my feet.

Since bait fish tend to work close to shore after dark when winged predators do not bother them, and since many of the groined beaches along our coasts are peopled with swimmers during the day, jetty jockeys are inclined to be people of the night. Standard equipment therefore includes a headlamp or some similar light-ing device. It is not worn on the head, however, but around the neck or even the waist. The reason: a wobbling light beam stabbing through the darkness may scare bluefish away. Blues are not normally alarmed by navigational lights, such as those found on buoys, which remain in one place. They can be spooked by erratic flashes. Therefore shield any light well and use it sparingly. A pencil flashlight held in the teeth serves well on the open beach when changing lures. I have never tried it on a jetty because I am afraid I might swallow it!

Casting, of course, is not limited to open beaches and jetties as a method of taking bluefish. Any platform, whether it is a boat, pier, bridge, tidal river bank, or bar will serve. When the fish have not been spotted visually and no tide rip is handy, I like to troll from a small boat until there is a strike. Then my choice is to kill the motor, drift or anchor, and go to work on the blues by casting. This system makes it possible to present a lure again and again to the quarry and, in nine cases out of ten, this system will get better results than straight trolling.

Be sure that you know your fellow anglers and that you have control of your own casts. Once while fishing with an angler—who shall be nameless—off the Florida coast near Stuart, I had my cap removed three times in ten minutes by a multi-hooked plug wielded by this character. I recommended in no uncertain terms that we start trolling. I do not feature being known along the coast as Old One-Eye. Boat casting can be perfectly safe when those involved know what they are doing. It can be extremely hazardous when they do not.

Ideally when in small craft, a right-handed and left-handed fisherman can work without any interference. Such combinations are rare. Two right-handers should fish with the man in the bow casting to port and the man in the stern,

Irv Sosin shows a bluefish he caught in Biscayne Bay while casting with light tackle from a boat.

to starboard. If both wish to cast to the same side, the bow man casting to starboard must be alert and careful; when both cast to port, the onus is on the stern man.

When a fish is hooked, it is polite to stop casting and allow the fortunate fisherman time to bring his catch alongside— polite, but not necessarily practical. Often blues will be moving fast and the opportunities for hooking them are few and far between. In addition, several bluefish may follow their hooked companion and will strike readily at a lure presented close by. Here, accuracy and skill become important. If a plug or other lure is dropped near the blue trying to escape, an explosive strike often follows. Lines may cross and both fish may be lost, yet this risk is worth taking, always providing the fishermen involved agree to such a procedure *before* leaving the dock.

Blues at times work into shallows where a boat may not travel safely. Casting is the answer. By lying off in deep water, lures may be presented readily and the craft itself will not spook the fish. Obviously under such conditions, the ability to throw a long line is an advantage. If fellow fishermen are on the beach casting seaward, move well out of range. Remember that shore-bound anglers have few choices among fishing areas while the boatman can cover a tremendous amount of water easily.

Once a school has sounded or disappeared, I prefer to stay in the same general area rather than to start trolling all over the ocean. Bluefish may travel fast, but bait schools normally move at a slower speed. Drifting with the current and casting at regular intervals off each side of the boat may relocate the feeding fish. If it does not, start the motor and move slowly, casting as before. When this fails, resume trolling at normal speed while using the retiring search plan described earlier.

This open-cockpit boat for offshore bluefishing allows plenty of room for casting.

From piers, catwalks along bridges, and the bridges themselves, casting may be severely limited due to the presence of many other fishermen. On many fishing piers, overhand or side casting is strictly prohibited as a very sound safety measure. Those who have mastered the underhand flip cast will be winners. This cast is not difficult once the angler realizes that the snap of the rod does the work.

With a short drop-off between rod tip and lure, bring the rod smartly forward as it points toward the water. Use wrist action only. Then snap it back so that the rod is fully flexed. Another snap forward as the line is released will send the lure on a path approximately parallel to the water. The distance cast is not great, yet it often is enough to place a lure where bluefish will grab it.

Those fishing off structures over the water have a special problem after the bluefish has been hooked and played to exhaustion. The angler is separated from his catch by a large expanse of open air below his feet. Small fish of course can be derricked up to land level, provided the tackle will take the strain. With larger specimens, there are two alternatives. The first is to lead the fish to the end of the pier or bridge and beach it in the shallows. This is often impossible, and is al-

It is possible to tail a bluefish in this manner without the aid of a gaff or net, but beware of those chopping teeth at the other end of the fish.

ways a nuisance. The second is to have a very long-handled net or gaff, or to have a net or weighted snatch-hook which may be lowered on a rope to lift the catch to safety. Most commercial fishing piers have such devices available.

For the fisherman who makes a business of pier and bridge angling, the snatch-hook is the easiest rig to carry. A commercial, treble-hooked cod jig tied to a length of stout cord will serve the purpose well.

While on this general subject, I should point out that gaffs and nets are standard equipment for bluefishermen, except for the surf caster, who seek big fish. Even some surf casters like to use a small belt gaff, but I must admit I do not. I prefer to beach the catch. On a jetty, however, a belt gaff comes in handy. Nets, unless they have metal mesh, will be chomped to pieces by bluefish. Be prepared for attrition, and make a point of getting the fish out of the net as quickly as possible. Boat gaffs, of course, should feature a handle long enough to reach the water without causing the gaffer to double up over the side so that his head is below his heels.

If it were possible, I would have all those who plan to net or gaff bluefish train with a pier net on a rope, or with a snatchhook. If this were done, it would become apparent to trainees that the catch must be led over the retrieving device. Neophytes are apt to lash about with either a net or gaff in an attempt to run the bluefish down. The term "brought to net" or "brought to gaff" means just that, and it is up to the angler to do the bringing.

Light tackle casting from shore is not only effective when after bluefish, but also provides excellent sport. More limited as far as maneuverability is concerned than his boating counterpart, the beach-bound angler still can cover a great deal of fish-holding water. Local knowledge of both coastline and bluefish habits in the area pay off. For example, a point on the seaward side of a tidal marsh may be little more than a mudflat at low tide, yet will be a prime feeding ground an hour before the top of the flood.

There are comparatively rare occasions when the light tackle man can outfish the surf caster facing the open ocean. These usually are when blues are chasing very small bait into the wash. A one-handed spinning or free-spool rod can present lures small enough to match the bait. Such tackle in the high surf also seems to be the answer when bluefish are feeding on sandeels, known also as launce. Although a sandeel may grow to be more than six inches in length, a tiny metal jig, spoon, or bucktail gets more strikes than a lure more closely simulating the natural bait. Please do not ask me why.

It is in the coastal estuaries and bays, however, that the light tackle shore caster comes into his own. When winds and seas rage along the open coast, almost always some sheltered nook can be found in the lee on what is termed inside waters. Here the angler can do much as the surf caster and jetty jockey does, only everything is in miniature except, perhaps, the fish themselves.

Because underwater—and even above water—obstructions are a particular hazard to light lines, it is always wise to follow the lead of bank burglars: case the joint before going into action. Make a mental note of just where the hazards lie so that, if a fish is hooked, you know when to put maximum pressure on it to prevent a cut-off. Also pick out for future reference a point along the bank or beach where the catch may be landed without too much trouble. Trying to reach a convenient little slope of sand, with an eight-pound bluefish leaping about on the end of an eight-pound line, can be frustrating if an eight-foot-deep mudhole lies between you and that landing point.

The general rules for all bluefish casting apply in light tackle work from shore. Try different speeds of retrieve, different depths, and different lures. In general, the rate at which the reel handle is turned should be considerably faster than that used when fishing with heavier gear from the surf or a boat. The lure itself will not move faster, since the reel spool is of smaller diameter and less line is recovered on each turn during the retrieve. Reels with a high retrieve ratio are favored for this method of angling.

As I have noted, bowing to a leaping bluefish when using fairly heavy tackle is a mistake. The fish will throw the hooks all too readily. With light tackle, the bow may be required to save a broken line. Bluefish still may throw the lure, but the lure's smaller size and smaller penetrating hooks are factors in the angler's favor. The risk of losing a fish is worth the chance of saving terminal tackle to my mind. I bow.

On the first run after a fish is hooked, it pays to copy the bonefisherman who wades the flats. Hold the rod well above your head so that the line runs clear of the bottom. The slightest touch against a stick, rock, or bit of shell when light line is scorching off the reel spells disaster. I have reeled in slack without the comforting resistance of a lure many times in such fishing, and undoubtedly will do so many times more. On each occasion, I try to analyze just what I did that was wrong and often find I have only myself to blame. Sometimes I have to come to the conclusion that the bluefish simply was smarter than I was, and I then wish the escaper well.

In light tackle casting, play each and every current variation to the fullest extent. It takes little effort to repeat a cast several times until the lure lands in exactly the right spot. As in jetty fishing, work the lure right up to your feet, for a strike may come just as the hook is being lifted clear of the water. If the fish can be seen approaching when this happens, you must have nerves of steel to resist the impulse to tweak the lure out of that slashing mouth. My nerves have yet to reach that stoic point, and I hope they never will!

The fly fisherman has a particular problem when after blues. Since he is dependent on stripping in line by hand rather than by retrieving by turning the reel handle, his lure moves at a rate that may have little appeal to his quarry. There are multiplying fly reels in which the reel spool turns twice or more with each turn of the handle, but these are designed basically to recover slack line during the battle. To cast, reel in all line, then strip it off the reel and cast again is a procedure that is both tedious and inefficient. A sure sign that a fly is not moving fast enough to bring a strike is when a

blue swims up behind it, looks cross-eyed at the feathers, and then turns away. Strong men have been known to become weak under such circumstances.

Raising the rod tip smartly may turn the trick. However, the speed imparted to the fly by this maneuver is only momentary, and there is slack line to recover when the rod tip is dropped again. During that period, the lure lies dead in the water. Fast stripping in of line is the basic answer. If you can coil this in one hand while stripping, you are better than I am. I coil the line at my feet and make sure that I have trampled down grass and sticks to make a special nest for it. It is the only solution I have found to date for fast stripping. Some claim a belt "basket" is the answer, but it is not for me. It is more of a hindrance than a help when I am trying to make that fly really move through the water. Pacific steelhead anglers who may turn to bluefishing probably will disagree, for they are accustomed to the rig.

Do not forget the technique used by George Bonbright off Great Point Rip on Nantucket. Dropping a fly within sight range of a bluefish—known or suspected to be present—time after time enrages the creature. A delicious tidbit falls from the sky, is available for a moment, then vanishes as suddenly as it came. On the third or fourth cast, the blue decides not to let it escape again, and the strike can be explosive. This trick works with a popping bug as well as with a streamer.

As is true with other methods of bluefishing, changing lures can mean the difference between little and plenty. Paul Kukonen found that a small fly cast into feeding blues walloping tiny menhaden would be hit immediately. Larger offerings were ignored. The small fly simulated the tiny bait and, by giving it a wounded, fluttering action, Paul matched the hatch and the action. Conditions, of course, had to be exactly right, and the fish had to be feeding within casting range.

Although fly fishermen hate to admit it, there are many times when their tackle simply will not reach the fish. A sneaky trick is to have a companion, armed with long-range gear, cast a hookless plug to sighted blues. As he retrieves the lure, blues will follow it and whack it again and again. Their temper seems to increase in direct proportion with the num-ber of times they fail to be caught. Enticed within fly casting range, the angler with the long wand can then go to work. A fly dropped near the moving plug will be gobbled down in short order.

Fly rods are not limited to fly lines. The late Leslie Thompson, artist and angler of Newton, Massachusetts, mounted a regular bait-casting reel loaded with light braid on the forward part of the butt on his fly rod. With this, he could flip a small

Frank Woolner strips in line to tempt a fly-rod bluefish at sundown.

natural or artificial bait an amazing distance. When he hooked a fish, he enjoyed maximum sport on the limber rod. The fact that it was limber also contributed to its ability to toss a soft, light silversides without danger of having it torn loose from the hook.

An adaptation of this same system became popular some years ago along the banks of the Cape Cod Canal. A standard single-action fly reel is loaded with light Dacron, to which is attached about 75 feet of eight- to ten-pound monofilament. The Dacron will not explode a reel spool as will monofilament alone. To the end of the mono is attached a short length of light wire or nylon-covered cable, then a light wire hook. The bait is any small minnow, speared through the eyes by the barb.

Where there is rubble underfoot, a line basket—which I avoid in regular fly fishing—is a necessity. The mono is stripped off the reel and is coiled carefully into the basket. If you do not have such a basket, a garbage pail lid at your feet will serve the purpose. Clamp the mono against the rod handle as when spinning, give the bait a gentle flip and it will travel through the air for a considerable distance. Retrieve, always making sure that the coils of mono are not crossed up. When a bluefish hits a bait presented in this manner, it engulfs it, so there is no trouble in setting the hook.

The trick during the battle is to get those coils of mono onto the reel without tangling, so that the fish may be fought without problems. The first rush of a blue normally takes care of this. Fight the quarry with a pumping action of the rod, for mono has stretch that must be overcome.

Why not use a regular spinning outfit for this fishing? The strain of the hook on a fragile bait at the start of the cast will tear the steel loose. A limber fly rod softens the shock.

Fly fishermen are inclined to state flatly that their method of angling is the most sporting there is, that it requires more skill than other alternatives, and that a fish therefore has a greater chance to escape. I agree that a leaping bluefish on a fly rod provides sport supreme. As far as skill is concerned, I disagree. Any neophyte may be taught to cast with a spinning outfit in a matter of minutes. That same potential angler may be taught to cast reasonably well with fly fishing tackle in an hour. To learn the same facility with a free-spool reel may take weeks, and there are some who never are able to master it.

As far as escape is concerned, again I disagree. Once solidly hooked on fly fishing tackle, a bluefish must drag a heavy, large-diameter line through the water. It will be fighting that line, as well as the flex of the rod, which, incidentally, is superbly designed to absorb sudden shocks. I do not belittle the fly rod, for it is one of my own favorite weapons. Jeff Dane, television outdoor star in Tidewater Virginia, used one to subdue a whopping 17 pound, 7 ounce bluefish off Virginia Beach on November 16, 1968, which gives an indication of what can be done with the long wand. However, it is specialized gear that can be used only when weather and water conditions are just right, and when the fish themselves swim within casting range. Like any other tackle, it has its limitations.

Bluefishing methods are not stereotyped. Those writing about blues tend to place these methods in categories, just as I have done. In actual angling practice, there is a great deal of overlap. An experienced fly fisherman instinctively casts his lure across a current and lets that current give the lure action and speed on the retrieve. A surf caster, fishing a bucktail, does the same. The chummer tries to attract bluefish within hooking range by laying down a stream of natural bait. The spin fisherman at the mouth of a tidal estuary lets Nature provide the chum, but his basic goal is identical. And so it goes.

If one method of bluefishing fails, try another. Experimentation throughout the ages has brought new refinements to old techniques, and will continue to do so. Watch a successful bluefisherman and try to learn from him. I have followed my own advice for more than 50 years, and I am still learning!

Same water, different tackle. Frank Woolner favors the fly-rod in this tidal estuary; the author tries his luck with light spinning gear.

5 / The Bottom of the Tackle Box

THROUGHOUT THIS VOLUME, I HAVE TRIED TO work in bits and pieces of general information in the various chapters. However, I find myself looking at a small heap of notes which were either forgotten or did not seem to fit conveniently into place. Scientists, when preparing papers, have a neat trick under such circumstances. They end their presentations with a section called "Conclusions" in which everything is wrapped up neatly and the desk cleared. Since I have no conclusions, this section must be considered a sort of catch-all, similar to the bottom of my tackle box after a week's fishing trip.

First, considering the bluefish itself, never forget that it is a voracious feeder and, as such, has incredibly strong digestive juices in its stomach. Left uncleaned without refrigeration for any length of time, it will literally digest itself. The entire body cavity contents will spoil in short order and the flesh will be tainted. Clean your catch as soon as possible.

On large sport fishing craft, a fish box partially filled with ice is standard equipment. On smaller boats, portable ice boxes serve well in keeping the catch cool. Lacking such conveniences, a burlap bag which has been moistened with sea water does a satisfactory job. Evapo-

Waders, pull-over parka, and long-billed cap are typical surf fishing garments. The parka is belted in the middle to provide a carrying strap for lures and also to keep waves from sneaking into the wader tops.

ration chills the contents, so keep the sack wet at all times. The beach fisherman may not even have a bag available. He can limit the ravages caused by hot sunlight by burying a bluefish whole in the sand. Never fail to mark the internment spot with a piece of driftwood or stone. Digging about like a dog seeking a buried bone can be the height of frustration.

If cleaning a blue on a sand beach, do the job on a piece of plank or similar clean surface. Sand grains otherwise will work their way into the flesh, which may help your local dentist at a later date, but may discourage the gourmet. Resident sea gulls will welcome the offal, but bluefish heads should be buried deep.

This is not a cookbook, so I do not intend to list all sorts of bluefish recipes. Cookbook authors do not tell me what tackle to use for bluefishing; therefore I steer clear of their area of endeavor in grateful acknowledgement of their forebearance in mine. However, it should be made clear that a bluefish filet spanking fresh makes a far better meal than one which has been lying around on ice for a long period of time. If the catch must be frozen, use the quick-freeze process, or place it in a container of slightly salted water prior to putting it in a home freezer.

This brings up the subject of salt water itself. In large quantities, as is the case in oceans, I find it extremely pleasant. In small, cold quantities, as in the case of leaking waders, it is the reverse. Charley Waterman of DeLand, Florida, who catches a good many fish in the course of a year and writes well about the catching, has an excellent trick which I have copied. When he buys a new pair of waders, he puts them on and then sits down in a bathtub full of water to browse through the evening paper. If there are any leaks, he discovers them under conditions that are comfortable, and in a situation where he can make repairs easily. I use the same system with old waders which have been hanging unused during the winter. Leaks found when standing waist deep in the surf, casting to slashing blues, can ruin a good day—or night. Incidentally, when storing waders for a long period of time, wash them well inside and out with fresh water, let them dry thoroughly and then hang them so that air may circulate through them.

Unless the weather is warm, when bathing trunks may be worn, waders are the choice for a surf caster. With a foul weather parka belted at the waist, an angler so equipped is almost watertight. Hip boots do not serve the purpose, although they may be adequate for walking the banks of a tidal estuary.

A long-billed cap, known to the trade as a Block Island swordfisherman's cap, is my choice for headgear. The visor keeps sun out of the eyes and the cap fits snugly even when the wind is brisk. Frank Woolner favors a beret when gales howl and he is welcome to his choice. When I wear a beret, I feel that something is nesting in my hair. Under tropic sun, a hat with a wide brim is advisable to keep the sun from crisping the tops of your ears. A length of line with a snap at each end— one snap for the hat and one for a shirt's buttonhole—will keep the hat from blowing out of reach.

As for the remainder of my fishing garb, I pick a long-sleeved shirt because the sleeves may be rolled down when the sun burns. Lightweight long trousers are chosen for the same reason, and I use them even when wading in the tropics and semi-tropics. On a boat, my shoes are the deck-gripping type; on the sand, they are crepe- or rubber-soled, for sand will fill in the many gripping surfaces of such styles as the Topsider line.

Polarized sun glasses should be standard equipment. Not only will they shield the eyes from the sun's glare, but also they will enable you to spot fish lying under the surface. A short piece of line taped to the

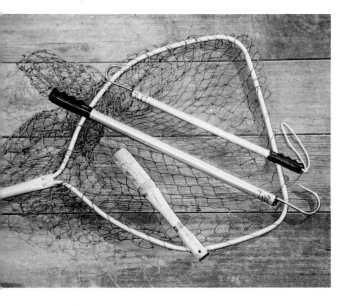

(Left) Use a net for trophies or for bluefish that are to be released. A short or long gaff is the choice when blues are to be boated and kept. A stout hammer-handled club will save finger bites.

A tackle box carries anything that is needed for bluefishing, from a good knife to extra spools of line, leaders, sinkers, hooks, lures, and tools for on-scene tackle repairs. Choose a well-made box designed for salt water use.

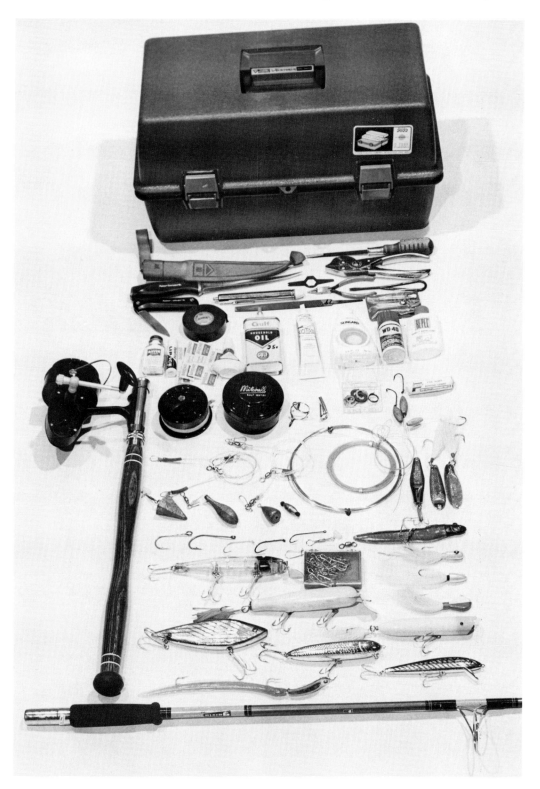

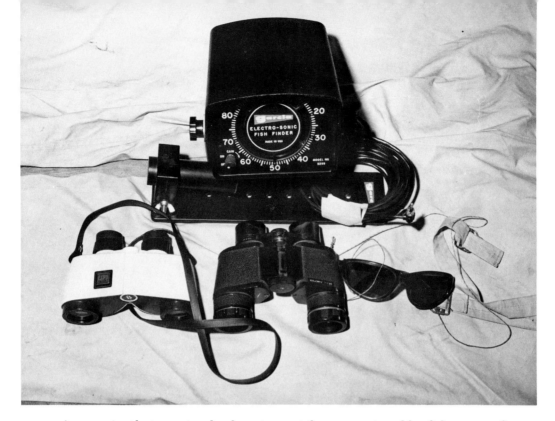

Accessories that are standard equipment for any serious bluefisherman afloat— depth-sounder, fish-finder, binoculars, and polarized sunglasses with a strap to keep them on your head and out of the water.

end of each bow and draped around the neck will keep them from slipping into the water.

Carrying extra lures and tackle replacements present no problem to the bluefisherman who uses a large boat for his sport. The small-craft angler is limited to some degree, but here again he can stow a good deal of gear in a regular salt water tackle box. For extra clothing, I recommend the waterproof ditty bags that may be found in any war surplus shop. For the shore fisherman, carrying lures and the like has always presented a problem. A tackle box located at the base of operations is all very well, but it is a nuisance when trying to cover a considerable stretch of beach.

Some use a shoulder bag. In my own experience, I have found this is fine when deep wading is not involved. However, if you have to go in over your knees, waves catch the bag at the most awkward moments and flip it into just the wrong spot and at the wrong moment. Carriers that

fasten to a belt are my choice. There are a few on the market, but I have yet to find a good one that will hold both large plugs and smaller tinclads. I therefore have fashioned one of my own, made from heavy canvas, and it has stood the test of time. If you are not accustomed to working with canvas, a local cobbler can do the work if supplied with a basic design.

As I have noted before, I do not use a gaff when surf-casting. When fishing the jetties, a belt gaff that doubles as a billy club does the trick. A billy club alone is useful both on the beach and afloat. An excellent way to lose fingers is to remove a plug from the snapping jaws of a very live bluefish. Conk the creature on the side of the head and you will then be able to proceed without being a candidate for the local hospital. Creasing a blue right across the skull does not seem to bother it very much.

Stout cutting pliers should be part of a bluefisherman's equipment not only for

Frank Woolner, Spider Andresen, Kib Bramhall, and Hal Lyman are dressed for the occasion—surf fishing.

snipping leaders, but also for clipping a hook shank when the barb is located in some place where it does not belong. A Band Aid or two is handy for minor first aid. Sunburn lotion also adds a bit of health insurance. My many medical friends tell me that amateur first aid often causes more trouble than the original injury, and I respect their opinions. Therefore, if you or your companion are hurt, head for the doctor as soon as possible.

As far as first aid for tackle is concerned, I always carry a spare rod tiptop of fairly large diameter. The tip can be built up with thread or fishing line to fit it, and ferrule cement, which melts when a match is applied, will secure the spare in place temporarily. Rod guides may be fashioned out of heavy leader wire in a pinch. A small roll of electrician's tape will hold them in place. This tape is good for dozens of other emergency repairs also. A bottle of clear nail polish is another good investment for touching up

frayed lures and rod windings.

In former times, a can of light oil was standard equipment in all tackle boxes. Today, this has been replaced to a large degree with a small spray can of the modern water-displacing lubricants, such as WD-40 and CRS. These space-age products can do wonders for a balky reel, as well as for the electrical system of a boat's engine drenched in fog. If you drop your reel in the sand—and everyone does it at some time—rinse it well in the cleanest part of the ocean nearby, then squirt it with one of these solutions. The reel may grind a bit for a moment, but will shortly perform as it should.

The advice old Captain Josiah Nickerson, now long dead, gave to young bluefishermen was: "Keep feathers clean, metal bright and hooks sharp." That advice is as good today as it was years ago.

Whether it was the good Captain's ancestor or not, I do not know, but there is an apocryphal tale concerning another

Cape Cod Nickerson which will underline my final point. Trolling from his catboat with a handline and a lead drail, he felt a tremendous strike, then the line went slack. Upon hauling in the lure, he found it bitten cleanly in two. Three days later on the same grounds, he caught a huge bluefish. When the catch was cleaned, sure enough, there was the tail end of the drail lodged in the fish's stomach! The lure must have been made of soft metal.

The point, of course, is that bluefish have sharp teeth and will use them. I have noted this before, and will underline the fact in conclusion, in the hope that the fingers you save will be your own.

As long as blues continue to use those teeth, to attack a lure or bait with unequalled savagery, to battle spectacularly for their freedom, to upset all the rules of behavior just when you think you have learned something about them, I hope to be able to totter to the edge of the sea in my quest for bluefish until I pass over the River Styx.

Who knows? There may be bluefish in the Styx itself. Then I will have one last chance for glory!